MO[

A Pictorial History
Ray Newell

VELOCE PUBLISHING
THE PUBLISHER OF FINE AUTOMOTIVE BOOKS

www.veloce.co.uk

First published in February 2021 by Veloce Publishing Limited, Veloce House, Parkway Farm Business Park, Middle Farm Way, Poundbury, Dorchester DT1 3AR, England. Tel +44 (0)1305 260068 / Fax 01305 250479 / e-mail info@veloce.co.uk / web www.veloce.co.uk or www.velocebooks.com.
ISBN: 978-1-787110-55-7; UPC: 6-36847-01055-3.

MORRIS CARS
1948 to 1984

A Pictorial History
Ray Newell

VELOCE

CONTENTS

A HISTORY OF MORRIS

The Morris marque, for so long a part of British motoring history, took its name from its founder William Richard Morris, born 1877. At the age of 14 William started work in the cycle trade, and in the years that followed pursued his passion as a keen amateur cyclist, winning many trials and distance events. Having served his apprenticeship, he set up his own cycle repair business in Oxford in 1896, before expanding to include motorcycle repairs in 1902. Automotive activities, including car repairs, a car hire business and operating a taxi service were to be the precursors to car sales and the acquisition of premises in 1910 in Longwall Road, Oxford. Morris harboured ideas of designing and building a car of his own, and so, in 1912, he registered a new company: WRM Motors Ltd. In March the following year his first car, the Morris Oxford Light Car, was offered for sale. The vehicle was a two seater powered by an 8.9hp engine, and cost £165.

Morris' business model was innovative and effective. Instead of tying up property and manpower in one location to produce all the components for the vehicle, he instead adopted a supply chain model utilising the expertise of other component manufacturers. In the case of the Morris Oxford, bodies were supplied by coachbuilder Charles Raworth and Sons, the chassis came courtesy of Rubery Owen brothers, axles and steering from EG Wrigley and Company Ltd, specially designed wheels from Sankey, and the engine, clutch and three-speed gearbox from White and Poppe. The distinctive radiator, destined to define the car as the 'Bullnose' Morris, was produced initially by the Coventry Motor Fittings company, and later by Doherty Motor Components.

Morris' optimism received a welcome boost with an initial order for 400 cars from Gordon Stewart, proprietor of the successful London-based Stewart and Arden motor vehicle distributor. In anticipation of volume sales, and the need for bigger premises, Morris moved his assembly plant to Cowley in Oxfordshire where, in the years that followed,

1913 Bullnose Morris at Nuffield Place.

millions of Morris cars were produced, and where, today, the BMW Mini is built (on part of the original site).

By 1914 six versions of the Morris Oxford, including a delivery van and a coupé, were on offer. However, momentum slowed due to the impact of the First World War and the requirement for premises to be given over to munitions production. Nevertheless, a new model, the Morris Cowley was introduced in 1915. It sported a body supplied by Hollick and Pratt and was powered by an American Continental U engine mated to a three-speed gearbox.

In 1919 Morris changed the name of the company to Morris Motors Ltd, and in the same year switched engine production to the French company Hotchkiss, utilising the engines built at its Coventry plant. In the aftermath of the First World War the British economy suffered a recession, and this impacted greatly on the British motor industry. Undeterred by declining sales, Morris took the unprecedented step of reducing the price of his cars. Remarkably sales increased, much to the chagrin of his competitors who were forced to follow suit. In another astute move, which was to have a major impact on the future of the company, Morris began the process of acquiring companies which had been his sub-contractors. Additions included body supplier Hollick and Pratt which he renamed 'Morris Bodies,' the Osberton Radiator Company which became Morris Radiators Ltd, Hotchkiss which became Morris Engines Ltd, and EG Wrigley Ltd which became 'Morris Commercial Cars.' Later, in 1926, the SU Carburettor Company was added to the portfolio, along with Wolseley Motors.

Ever mindful of automotive developments elsewhere William Morris travelled abroad and, following a visit to the USA to explore all-steel body production methods, he entered into a collaborative venture with Edward G Budd to establish the Pressed Steel Company in Cowley. Morris' influence on the British Motor industry was expanding along with his business interests, but there was still the serious business of developing new models and competing in a marketplace faced with challenging economic circumstances. Morris Oxford and Cowley models continued to be produced side by side, but in 1927, the 'Flatnosed' Morris Oxford, so called because of the more modern styled radiator, was introduced. The model range was expanded with a 16hp Morris Oxford and an 18hp Light Six being added. Attention was also being given to the development of a smaller range of cars. The acquisition of Wolseley Motors in 1927 presented the opportunity to further develop an existing 8hp overhead camshaft engine. This led to Morris entering the 8hp class with the Morris Minor in 1929. Priced at £125, it was promoted as being capable of 50mph and 50mpg. The 1929 slump and the depression of the early 1930s impacted greatly on the sales of larger cars, and Morris, aware of financial limitations, introduced the £100 car. A side-valve engine was fitted to the Morris Minor to reduce costs, and, in a clever advertising ploy, the car was advertised as a £100 car capable of 100mph and

The pre-war Morris Minor achieved fame as the £100 Morris car.

100mpg. In 1931 both feats were achieved in two separate staged events – 100mph at Brooklands in a supercharged model, and 100mpg during a controlled economy run.

Although the Morris Minor faced stiff competition from the well-established Austin Seven introduced in 1922, sales held up well ... During the 1930s Morris introduced several other models, including 16hp and 25hp models of the Oxford, and boasted models in 8, 10, 12, 14, 16, 18 and 25hp sectors. The foothold in the small car sector was consolidated in 1934 when the Series 1 Morris Eight was introduced, and the innovative nature of Morris Cars was showcased with the launch of the Morris M Ten, the first Morris model to feature mono-construction. In 1935 Morris Motors claimed to be the first automotive company to effectively introduce 'specialisation.' This, according to the in-house promotion material, was the process by which "... one factory produces nothing but engine ... another concerns itself solely with foundry work ... a third concentrates on radiators ... a fourth is devoted entirely to coachwork. The products of these four specialised factories are then assembled at Cowley in the largest and best equipped motorcar assembly plant in Britain." It was an innovative undertaking which helped Morris to reach total sales of one million vehicles by 1939. However, within months the plant at Cowley had been given over to the war effort. Thousands of damaged aircraft were repaired there and returned to the fray.

In the immediate postwar era, and under the vice-chairmanship of Miles Thomas, development work began on a new range of small, intermediate and large Morris cars. When launched at the 1948 London Motor Show, designer Alec Issigonis took the plaudits for the innovative design of the Morris Minor Series MM and Morris Oxford MO models in particular. Monocoque construction was in vogue, and along with independent front suspension, torsion bar springing and more modern body styling, set the scene for car production from that point on. The need to increase export sales in order to revitalise the British economy after the war prompted the building of a new CKD facility at Cowley in 1950. The Nuffield Organisation which included Morris, Wolseley, Riley, MG Cars and Morris Commercial Vehicles led the way in the postwar 'Export or Die' campaign.

An artist's impression of post-war Morris Minor, Cowley, Oxford and Isis models, all of which are covered in this publication.

A significant development in the history of Morris occurred in 1952 when Morris Motors Ltd and the Austin Motor Company – for so long bitter rivals – merged to form the British Motor Corporation Ltd. The new company, referred to as BMC, immediately became the largest manufacturer of cars and commercial vehicles in Britain, and the fourth largest in the world. Morris, by way of the Nuffield Organisation, already had contracts with established large scale overseas plants and, under the banner of BMC, assembly of CKD Morris cars continued in Ireland, the Netherlands, Sweden, South Africa, India, Australia and New Zealand.

Collaborative marketing saw many Austin and Morris vehicles being subjected to badge engineering with, in some cases, Wolseley and Riley variants being added to the range. In part this was to satisfy the marque loyalty which still existed, particularly between Austin and Morris customers, some of whom, like the employees who worked for the respective companies, were never accepting of the BMC merger. When, in 1968, BMC merged with the Leyland Motor Company to form British Leyland, 'Austin-Morris' retained its identity within the group. Riley disappeared in 1969 and Wolseley soldiered on until 1975. During the British Leyland era, which saw Triumph and MG come under the company umbrella, badge engineering continued. The exceptions were the Morris Marina and the Morris Ital, both of which retained their exclusive Morris identity. The last 'hurrah' for the 'Morris' name came, somewhat ironically, via the Austin Metro, introduced in 1980. In 1982 when a van version of the Metro was introduced to the range the decision was taken to market it as a Morris Metro. Later the designation changed to Austin with 310 models being

First and last Morris cars: an Ital and a Bullnose photographed on the occasion of the centenary of Morris in 2013 in Oxford.

available. Towards the end of production they were simply known as Metrovans. So far as car production was concerned the Ital models were the last to carry the Morris name. Production ended in 1984.

William Richard Morris was a high profile figure during his lifetime. Apart from his success with the companies which bore his name, he secured a well-deserved reputation as a philanthropist, giving generously to science, medicine, education and social care. He was given a peerage in 1934 and took the title Lord Nuffield. In 1938 he became a Viscount. He died in 1963 aged 85. It is estimated that in his lifetime his bequests totalled £30,000,000. As Nuffield his name will be familiar to many who visit hospitals and other institutions which benefitted from his generosity, and for those with an interest in things automotive, Morris remains a well-respected British marque.

One can only speculate on what Lord Nuffield would make of the latest proposals linking his name to a new 21st century vehicle. In 2019/2020 the Morris name once more came to prominence, and if planned developments continue it will feature on a

William Morris (Lord Nuffield) pictured in the grounds of Nuffield Place.

technologically advanced electric commercial vehicle by 2021. The Morris Commercial trade name was acquired by the state-owned Chinese car maker SAIC in 2007. Pre-production vehicles based on the iconic 1949 Morris J type van were unveiled in 2019. Production of the Morris Commercial JE van will be based in Worcestershire,

England. Initially this will focus on the JE type van, but pick-up and minibus versions may follow depending on the success of the venture. The essential features of the original J type are inherent in the design of the new JE model which will feature a lightweight modular chassis, carbon fibre panels, and will be powered by British produced lithium ion batteries. Its existence offers the prospect of a range of Morris-badged commercial vehicles suited to 21st century motoring returning to the road.

2019 Morris JE van. A Morris for the 21st century.

ACKNOWLEDGEMENTS

Compiling all the information for this book has been a challenge as well as a pleasure. Meeting with various owners and enthusiasts with a particular interest in Morris cars has not only broadened my own knowledge but given a wider insight into the clubs which cater for the different Morris models.

First and foremost, I must record my thanks to David Rowe, author of several titles in the Veloce Pictorial History series. His encouragement, unstinting support and practical assistance in providing information and photographic images has been invaluable. I am also indebted to several club officials who have given freely of their time to answer queries, confirm facts, source photographs, and liaise with owners of specific vehicles. In this regard I am particularly grateful to Cameron Shaw, John Weir, Chris Morris, Clive Serrell, Dr Martin Nancekievill, Trevor Ford and Brian Ford.

Many other enthusiasts have either made their vehicles available to be photographed or supplied specific images. Thanks are due to:

Paul Temple, Frank Mc Donagh, John Colley, Brian Wood, Sandy Hamilton, Andy Walker, Jason Thorne, James Hinnells, Martin Flanders, Rob Symonds, David Robinson, Howard Dent, John Carroll, Ian Potter, David Rippard, Rob Sibson, Tom Morley, Gordon Diffey, Mervyn Irvine, Steve Lee, Dawn Kennedy, Nick Basford, Paul Gordon, John Price, John Lakey, Mark Sutcliffe, Eddie Foster, Paul Keld, Brian Watkinson, Rick Beardmore, Chris Weedon, Brendan Symington, Roy Sawtell, Cain Hagan and the press office at the British Motor Museum.

Thanks, are also due to Kevin Quinn and the staff at Veloce Publishing who have worked to produce this book in the most trying of circumstances during 2020.

Ray Newell
Loscoe, Derbyshire

Morris Minor Series MM

In the immediate aftermath of the Second World War Morris Minor Ltd introduced a new model range at the Earls Court Motor Show in 1948. The undoubted star of the show was the Alec Issigonis-designed Morris Minor, available as a two-door saloon and a two-door open-topped Tourer. They were accompanied by the Morris Oxford and Morris Six models. These innovative models stood apart from their predecessors in many respects. The Morris Minor was of monocoque design and featured an all-steel chassis-less structure with a turret top roof and one-piece floor pressing on the saloon version. Independent front suspension, rack and pinion steering, 14in wheels and flowing body lines combined to create a small car with many attractive attributes, not least of which was the aesthetically pleasing, comfortable, and well-appointed interior,

Upwards of 80% of early cars went for export, either as complete vehicles or as CKD (Completely Knocked Down) for assembly overseas.

Two types of rear light were fitted to the Series MM. Early (left); later (right).

Instrument layout.

American lighting regulations forced an early rethink on the design of the front wings.

enhanced by a choice of bright external paint colours. Not all Issigonis' planned innovations came to fruition, though.

11

Gearchange diagram.

Experiments with 800cc and 1100cc flat-four engine configurations which were trialled in prototype models came to nothing, and resulted in an updated version of the 918 side-valve engine used in the Morris 8 Series E being utilised in production models. This tried and tested power unit proved reliable and produced modest performance levels of 27bhp and a maximum speed of 62mph. Expectations were high that the new small car would prove popular in overseas markets, and that sales would contribute significantly to the British postwar economy. However, one unforeseen consequence of this ambition was to have a significant long-term effect on the external design of the Morris Minor. Lighting regulations in the State of California forced a radical change to the front wing design. Issigonis' favoured low headlamp arrangement had to be changed for the US market. Instead, 7in headlamps had to be incorporated into the front wings. Though initially adopted for overseas markets, particularly the USA, the new design was incorporated into the specification for the new four-door saloon announced in September 1950, and for all models from January 1951. During 1951 the introduction of fixed rear side windows instead of detachable side screens resulted in the designation of the open-topped models being changed from 'Tourer' to 'Convertible.' In the same year a nickel shortage prompted the introduction of a painted radiator grille and painted plain hub caps as an interim measure. Though chromium plated hub caps made a welcome return, the chromium radiator grille insert remained available only as an option. The Series MM model range continued in production until February 1953.

PRODUCTION NUMBERS: 176,002.
PRICES ON INTRODUCTION: Saloon £358, Tourer £358.
COLOURS ON INTRODUCTION: Black, Platinum Grey, Romain Green.
COLOURS THROUGHOUT PRODUCTION: Black, Platinum Grey, Romain Green, Maroon 'A', Mist Green, Gascoyne Grey, Thames Blue, Clarendon Grey, Empire Green, Birch Grey, Maroon 'B'.
OPTIONAL EXTRAS: HMV radio £42 16s 1d. Heater (fitted) £13 8s 4d.
ENGINE: Designated type USHM2. Cast iron block and head, four cylinders, in line, side-valve. Bore 57mm, stroke 90mm, 918cc. Maximum bhp 27.5 at 4400rpm. SU horizontal type H1 carburettor.
GEARBOX: Four-speed gearbox bolted to rear engine plate. Synchromesh on second, third and top gears. Clutch: Borg & Beck 6¼in (158.7mm) dry plate type AG. Ratios: reverse 3.95:1, first 3.95:1, second 2.30:1, third 1.54:1, top 1.00:1.
REAR AXLE: Semi-floating hypoid axle, ratio 9:41.
STEERING: Rack and pinion, 2.5 turns lock-to-lock.
BRAKES: Lockheed hydraulic 7in diameter drums (17.8cm). Front: two leading shoes. Rear: one leading and one trailing shoe.
TYRES: 14in (35cm) pressed steel disc. Four-bolt fixings. Tyres 5.00x14.
SUSPENSION: Front: Independent by torsion bars and links. Armstrong double-acting hydraulic dampers. Rear: Semi-elliptic leaf springs. Armstrong double-acting hydraulic dampers.
DIMENSIONS: Length: two-door saloon, Tourer and four-door saloon 12ft 4in (376cm); **height:** two-door saloon, four-door saloon 5ft 0in (152cm), Tourer 4ft 9in (143cm); **width:** all models 5ft 1in (155cm); **weight:** two-door saloon (15½cwt), Tourer (14cwt), four-door saloon (15¾cwt); **turning circle:** RH 33ft 1in (10.09m), LH 32ft 11in (10.04m).
CAPACITIES: Fuel: 5 gallons (23 litres). Boot: saloon, Tourer/convertible 7.8ft^3.

Morris Minor Series II

Developments at boardroom level in 1952 were destined to have a significant impact on the Morris Minor. The merger

Early (top) and late (lower) Series II Travellers.

of the Nuffield Organisation and the Austin Motor Company to form the British Motor Corporation (BMC) brought about tangible results, with the Austin 803cc overhead valve engine and accompanying gearbox being assigned for use in the Morris Minor. For a time, Series MM four-door models using the 918cc side-valve engines and Series II four-door models with the 803cc engine were built alongside each other at the Cowley Works. The only external distinguishing feature was a changed bonnet badge arrangement. Once Series MM production ceased in 1953 the Series II emerged as a model in its own right, with two-door, four-door, and convertible models acquiring the Series II specification. In October 1953 the Morris Minor Travellers' Car joined the range, at first being marketed as a Station Wagon. These ash-framed estate cars with aluminium rear roof section, side, and rear door panels were promoted alongside the larger Morris Oxford Series MO Traveller which had entered production in 1952. Early variants of the Series II models retained the same dashboard arrangement and early style 'cheese grater' front grille arrangement

The bonnet motif was the only external distinguishing feature between late Series MM and early Series II models.

as the Series MMs. In September 1954 a significant makeover occurred, though the mechanical specifications remained largely unchanged. The most striking change was the revised front-end arrangement which included horizontal grille bars and a repositioning of the sidelights. New-style rear lights with a built-in reflector and new chrome bezel were introduced. The most significant internal change focused on the dashboard. There, a new centrally located speedometer with open glove boxes either side, coupled with new-style seats with

fluted panels completed the revamp. With relatively little change, the Series II models remained in production until October 1956.

PRODUCTION NUMBERS: 269,838.
PRICE ON INTRODUCTION: Traveller 1953 standard £599, deluxe £622, 1953 four-door saloon £631, 1954 two-door saloon £529.
COLOURS ON INTRODUCTION: Maroon, Black, Clarendon Grey, Empire Green, Birch Grey.
COLOURS THROUGHOUT PRODUCTION: Maroon, Black, Clarendon Grey, Empire Green,

(Above) Fixed rear side windows were a feature of convertible models. Tourer models had detachable side screens.

A-series 803cc engine.

Instrument layout (later cars).

Birch Grey, Smoke Blue, Sandy Beige, Dark Green, Sage Green.

OPTIONAL EXTRAS: (1953 four-door saloon): Radio £25 2s 6d. Heater £10 10s 0d.

DELUXE SPECIFICATIONS: (Late Series II, Traveller, convertible and saloon): passenger sun visor, leather-covered seat cushions and squabs, front bumper over-riders, heater equipment on home models. Twin horns, sealed beam lamps, and induction heaters were standard equipment on North American market vehicles.

ENGINE: Cast iron block and head. Pressed steel sump. Four cylinders. Bore 58mm, stroke 76mm, 803cc. Maximum bhp 30 at 4800rpm. SU type H carburettor (1¼in).

GEARBOX: Four-speed gearbox bolted to rear engine plate. Synchromesh on second, third and top gears. Clutch: Borg & Beck 6¼in (158.7mm) dry plate. Ratios: reverse 5.174:1, first 4.09:1, second 2.588:1, third 1.679:1, top 1.000:1.

REAR AXLE: Hypoid axle, ratio 5.29:1 (7/37).

BRAKES: Lockheed hydraulic 7in diameter drums (17.8cm). Front: two leading shoes. Rear: one leading and one trailing shoe.

STEERING: Rack and pinion, 2.5 turns lock-to-lock.

TYRES: 14in (35cm) pressed steel disc. Four-bolt fixings. Tyres 5.00x14.

SUSPENSION: Front: Independent by torsion bars and links. Rear: Half elliptic leaf springs.

DIMENSIONS: Length: Two-door saloon, four-door saloon, convertible 12ft 4in (3.76m), Traveller 12ft 5in (3.79m); **height**: 5ft 0in (1.52m) all models; **width**: 5ft 1in (1.55m) all models; **turning circle**: 33ft (10m); **weight**: two-door saloon (15½cwt), four-door saloon

Gearchange diagram.

Saloon and convertible rear light arrangement.

(15¾cwt), convertible (15cwt), Traveller (16½cwt).

Traveller rear light arrangement.

CAPACITIES: Fuel: 5 gallons (30 litres).

Boot: saloons and convertibles 7.8ft³, Traveller 18ft-33ft³.

Morris Minor 1000 (948cc)

The success of the Morris Minor in terms of overseas and home market sales prompted thoughts of further restyling as early as 1955. Experimental work on a project codenamed DO1076 resulted in improved styling, a reworked interior, and an upgraded and much improved mechanical package which enhanced overall performance. The principal changes centred on the external body styling. All round visibility was improved, particularly on saloon models, with the decision to redesign the roof section. Larger front and rear screens combined with narrower front windscreen pillars along with fuller rear wings which enclosed more of the wheel resulted in a cleaner, sharper, more modern look. These changes were accompanied by interior refinements centred mainly

1957 Morris 1000 Saloon.

on the fascia, which retained the central speedometer, albeit with lidded glove boxes either side. Other changes for 1956/57 included a black, three-spoked, dished safety steering wheel and slightly revised seating with contrast piping. However, the most significant changes related to the mechanical specifications, which, in the unanimous opinion of contemporary road testers, transformed the car. The 948cc overhead valve engine coupled with a stronger slicker four-speed gearbox with

From August 1961, flashing indicators operated via the front sidelights and the rear lamps on home market models.

During 948cc production, the fascia layout changed from open glove boxes to lidded ones.

were replaced by flashing indicators in 1961, with the indicators being operated by a relay mounted in the engine bay. This allowed for 'American' style indication via larger plain front sidelights, and in combination with the rear brake lights. Fascia arrangements changed mainly due to an on/off arrangement with open and closed glove boxes.

THE MINOR MILLION

A significant landmark was reached in 1961 when sales of all variants of the Morris Minor reached one million. This was the first time this had been achieved by a British manufacturer. To mark the occasion, a limited edition 948cc Morris 1000 designated the Minor Million was produced in a striking lilac colour. It was badged appropriately and was fitted with a 'white gold' leather interior, black carpets, and special wheel rim embellishers. All 349 replicas were produced following the completion of the millionth vehicle.

349 distinctive replica models were produced to mark production of the millionth Morris Minor in 1961.

stronger synchromesh and a remote-control extension, provided for a much-improved driving experience. Better acceleration through the gears and a higher top speed added to the pleasure of driving a car already renowned for its handling. The mechanical upgrade remained in use until 1962. In the intervening years the main changes to specifications related to lighting, interior trim, and external body colours. Three distinct trim combinations featured in 984cc Morris 1000 models, the last of which was the duo-tone combination, available in red, green, and blue options with a contrasting silver beige insert on deluxe models. Semaphore indicators

Early Morris 1000 instrument layout (1956/7).

Gearchange diagram.

Later type instrument layout with central main beam warning light.

Morris 1000 948cc engine.

PRODUCTION NUMBERS: 544,048.
PRICE ON INTRODUCTION: Two-door saloon standard £590, deluxe £618. Four-door saloon standard £625, deluxe £659. Convertible standard £590, deluxe £618. Traveller standard £669, deluxe £696.
COLOURS THROUGHOUT 948CC PRODUCTION: Black, Dark Green, Clarendon Grey, Birch Grey, Sage Green, Cream*, Turquoise*, Pale Ivory*, Frilford Grey, Pearl Grey*, Clipper Blue, Smoke Grey, Yukon Grey, Old English White, Porcelain Green*, Lilac, Dove Grey*, Rose Taupe, Almond Green, Highway Yellow*, Trafalgar Blue.
* Indicates the colour was not used on the Traveller. Lilac was also used for the Minor Million only.
ENGINE: Cast iron block and head. Pressed-steel sump. Four cylinders set in line with overhead, pushrod-operated valves. Bore 62.9mm, stroke 76.2mm, 948cc. Maximum bhp 37 at 4750rpm. SU H2 type carburettor (1¼in).
GEARBOX: Four-speed gearbox bolted to rear engine plate. Remote control gearchange.

Synchromesh on second, third, and top gears. Clutch: Borg & Beck 6¼in (158.7mm) dry plate. Ratios: reverse 4.664:1, first 3.628:1, second 2.374:1, third 1.412:1, top 1.000:1.
REAR AXLE: Three-quarter floating rear axle, hypoid final drive, ratio. 4.55:1.
BRAKES: Lockheed hydraulic 7in diameter drums (17.8cm). Front: two leading shoes. Rear: one leading and one trailing shoe.
STEERING: Rack and pinion, 2.5 turns lock-to-lock.
TYRES: 14in (35cm) pressed-steel disc. Four-stud fixings. 5.00x14 tubeless.
SUSPENSION: Front: Independent by torsion bars and links. Rear: Half-elliptic leaf springs.
DIMENSIONS: Length: two-door saloon,

four-door saloon, convertible 12ft 4in (3.76m), Traveller 12ft 5in (3.79m); **height**: 5ft 0in (1.52m) all models; **width**: 5ft1in (1.55m) all models; **turning circle**: 33ft (10m); **weight**: two-door saloon (15½cwt), four-door saloon (15¾cwt), convertible (15cwt), Traveller (16½cwt).
CAPACITIES: Fuel: 6½ gallons (30 litres) from 1957. Boot: saloons and convertibles 7.8ft³, Traveller 18-33ft³.

Morris Minor 1000 (1098cc)

1962 brought further mechanical changes for the Morris Minor range when the 1098cc version of the A series engine was

1963 saloon. Note the 'clap hands' windscreen wiper arrangement.

Convertibles were the first Morris Minors to be discontinued (1969).

added to the specification. Accompanied by a different gearbox with baulk ring synchromesh on the top three gears, and a larger, stronger clutch and higher gearing, 4.22:1 as opposed to 4.55:1, overall performance was improved. Braking was enhanced by the introduction of 8in drum

brakes on the front. Trim, lighting, and body styling all remained as it had been on the previous 948cc Morris 1000 models until 1964, when what was to prove to be the last major revamp for the Morris Minor occurred.

Exterior changes centred on revised lighting with larger combined indicator and sidelight units on the front, and more imposing combined brake indicator and rear light units on the rear. The main changes that defined

Travellers, along with the light commercial vehicles, were the last Morris Minor models to be produced.

Gearchange layout.

*Instrument layout
(later cars).*

*Lighting arrangements: (above) all models,
front; (above right) saloon and convertibles
rear; (right) Traveller rear.*

the last series of Morris Minors related to the interior trim, a changed dash arrangement and a new-style steering wheel. Single-coloured heat-formed vinyl seat coverings and door trims provided a more modern look, and were complemented by a new-style dash panel with an anodised backing panel, a black faced speedometer, and a lidded passenger-side glove box.

Production continued with the whole model range after the British Motor Corporation was subsumed within British Leyland Motor Company BLMC in 1968. Soon after, though, consideration was given to the long-term future of the Morris Minor, and the demise of the Convertible models in June 1969 signalled the beginning of the end. Two-door and four-door models followed in November 1970. Traveller models along with light commercial variants remained in production at Adderley Park, Birmingham. Traveller production ended in April 1971, but light commercials continued until late 1971 by which time a total of 1.6 million of all types had been built.

PRODUCTION NUMBERS: 332,117.
PRICE ON INTRODUCTION: 1962. Two-door saloon. Standard £608, deluxe £637, four-door saloon standard £644, deluxe £679, convertible standard £608, deluxe £637, Traveller standard £689, deluxe £717.
COLOURS DURING PRODUCTION: (All models) Black, Smoke Grey, Old English White, Dove Grey, Rose Taupe, Almond Green, Trafalgar Blue, Maroon 'B', Peat Brown, Snowberry White.
Traveller only 1969/70: Blue Royale, Faun Brown, Cumulus Grey, Connaught Green, Glacier White, Bermuda Blue, White. June 1970/1971 : Aqua, Limeflower, Glacier White, Bedouin, Teal Blue, Bermuda Blue.
ENGINE: Cast iron block and head. Pressed

steel sump. Four cylinders set in line with overhead, pushrod-operated valves. Bore 64.58mm, stroke 83.72mm, 1098cc. Maximum bhp 48 at 5100rpm. SU HS2 carburettor (1¼in).
GEARBOX: Four-speed gearbox bolted to rear engine plate. Remote control gearchange. Synchromesh on second, third and top gears. Clutch: 7.25in single dry plate. Ratios: reverse 4.664:1, first 3.628:1, second 2.172:1, third 1.412:1, top 1.000:1.
REAR AXLE: Three-quarter floating rear axle. Hypoid final drive 4.22:1.
BRAKES: Lockheed hydraulic front 8in diameter drums, rear 7in diameter drums. Front: two leading shoes. Rear: one leading and one trailing shoe.
STEERING: Rack and pinion, 2.5 turns lock-to-lock.
TYRES: 14in (35cm) pressed-steel disc. Four-bolt fixings. Tyres 5.00x14 tubeless.
SUSPENSION: Front: Independent by torsion bars and links. Rear: Half elliptic leaf springs.
DIMENSIONS: Length: two-door saloon, four-door saloon, convertible 12ft 4in(3.76m), Traveller 12ft 5in (3.79m); **height**: 5ft 0in (1.52m) all models; **width**: 5ft 1in (1.55m) all models; **turning circle**: 33ft (10m); **weight**: two-door saloon (15½cwt), four-door saloon (15¾cwt), convertible (15cwt), Traveller (16½cwt).

CAPACITIES: Fuel: 6½ gallons (30 litres). Boot: saloons and convertibles 7.8ft³, Traveller 18-33ft³.

Morris Oxford Series MO

Announced in 1948 at the same time as the Morris Minor, the Morris Oxford Series MO shared many similar features. Body styling from the windscreen rearwards, while larger scale, was from the same template. The frontal arrangement was dominated by a large, one-piece grille panel, a one-piece chrome front bumper, and high headlamps integrated into the front wings. Internal arrangements were generously proportioned, a leather faced bench-type front seat and a vinyl covered rear seat together provided comfortable seating for five people. The fascia housed a well-equipped instrument panel comprising a central speedometer, electric clock, an ammeter, oil pressure gauge, and a fuel gauge. These were flanked by a plain panel forward of the driver and a passenger glove box lid. There was a 16½in (42cm) spring arm steering wheel with column gearchange. The handbrake lever and a full-width parcel shelf were beneath the dashboard.
Production centred exclusively on the

Early Morris Oxford Series MO had contoured front edge with pointed ends and flat grille panel.

Later Morris Oxford Series MO with straight bonnet edge and more prominent grille panel.

four-door saloon models until the Series MO Traveller joined the model range in 1952. External body styling changes between 1948 and 1952 centred on the bonnet, grille, and lighting changes, the most significant being the replacement of the original contoured style bonnet with the pointed edges to a straight-edged bonnet and revised front grille panel in 1949, and the introduction of the imposing stainless-steel grille panel in 1952.

Mechanical changes during production were minimal, particularly with regard to the durable 1476cc side-valve engine. Apart from a revised pressurised cooling system, the introduction of a larger radiator and the repositioning of the SU fuel pump away from the original location close to the exhaust manifold to reduce fuel vaporisation

The dark crinkle finish on early dashboards was replaced by smooth gold paint on later models.

problems little changed. Improvements to the suspension came courtesy of rear telescopic shock absorbers in place of the earlier level arm type dampers. Tyres were of larger section, increased from 5.25 to 5.50. Optional extras at launch included a heater, radio and over-riders.

The Morris Oxford Series MO sold well and was a popular export model. Like the Morris Minor it was exported in large numbers as complete cars, as well as being assembled from CKD (completely knocked down) kits in established overseas assembly plants. In India the Morris Oxford was built and sold as the Hindustan 14. Production of the Morris Oxford Series MO ended in early 1954.

PRODUCTION NUMBERS: 154,932.
PRICE ON INTRODUCTION: October 1948 £505. December 1951 £698.
COLOURS ON INTRODUCTION: Romain Green, Platinum Grey, Black.
COLOURS THROUGHOUT PRODUCTION: Romain Green, Platinum Grey, Black, Maroon, Thames Blue, Mist Green, Gasgoyne Grey, Clarendon Grey, Birch Grey and Empire Green.
ENGINE: Cast iron block and head. Four-cylinder side-valve engine. Bore 73.5mm, stroke 87mm, 1476.5cc. Maximum bhp 41 at 4000rpm. SU H2 (1¼in) carburettor.
GEARBOX: Four-speed gearbox, bolted to rear engine plate. Synchromesh on second, third and top gears. Column-mounted gearchange. Clutch: 7¼in single dry plate. Ratios: reverse 18.56:1, first 18.56:1, second 10.98:1, third 7.342:1, top 4.875:1.
REAR AXLE: Semi-floating hypoid bevel.

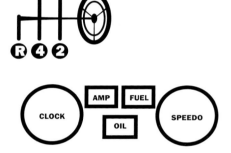

Gearchange diagram.

Instrument layout.

Ratios 4.55:1 (9/41) then 4.875:1 (8/39).
BRAKES: Lockheed hydraulic front and rear 8in diameter drums. Front: two leading shoes. Rear: one leading and one trailing shoe.
STEERING: Rack and pinion, 3 turns lock-to-lock.
TYRES: 5.25x15 bolt-on steel disc wheels. Later changed to 5.50x15 with 5-stud fixings.
SUSPENSION: Front: Independent with torsion bars and links. Rear: Semi-elliptic leaf springs. Hydraulic shock absorbers front and rear.
DIMENSIONS: **Length**: 13ft 11in (4.242m); **height**: 5ft 3in (1.600m); **width**: 5ft 5in (1.651m); **turning circle**: 36ft (11m).
Capacities: Fuel: 9 gallons. Boot: 9.9ft³.

Morris Oxford Series MO Travellers' Car

Introduced in September 1952, the Morris Oxford Series MO Travellers'

24

The Morris Oxford Series MO Travellers' Car pre-dated its Morris Minor counterpart by a year.

Car represented a departure from the monocoque body design of the Morris Oxford Series MO saloon. Although identical in terms of the body forward of the 'B' posts, a rear chassis frame supported an ash frame on to which weight saving aluminium sections were fitted to the sides and the lower sections of the two rear doors. A full-length aluminium roof panel was affixed rearward of the 'B' posts. Provision was also made for sliding windows on both sides of the ash frame.

The result was a roomy, multi-purpose vehicle officially designated as a Travellers' Car. However, it was also referred to as a 'Shooting Brake,' and in literature designed for the American market was classed as a 'Station Wagon.'

At launch the early models sported the earlier-type Mazak front grille, but this was soon dispensed with in favour of the stainless-steel version used on the saloon models. From 1953 the Travellers' Car was jointly marketed with the smaller Morris Minor version of the same model. Mechanically, the specification mirrored that of the saloon models. The main attraction of the vehicle was its capacious load-carrying potential. The option to pull the rear seat base forward, and then to push the split back squabs forward to create an enlarged flat floor area, was a real boon to commercial business travellers and family members alike. As if to stress the functionality of the vehicle, a durable floor covering in the form of a one-piece rubber mat was fitted to the passenger area. Standard and deluxe models were available. Deluxe models in 1953 benefitted from leather-covered seat cushions and squabs, and a 3½ kilowatt heating and ventilation system. Production continued until

Split front seats were used on the Travellers' Car to facilitate easier access to the rear seat.

March 1954. The Series MO Travellers' Car was superseded by the Series II Traveller in October 1954.

PRODUCTION NUMBERS: 5500.
PRICE ON INTRODUCTION: 1952 £825.
COLOURS THROUGHOUT PRODUCTION:
Clarendon Grey with maroon upholstery, Birch Grey with maroon upholstery, Empire Green with green upholstery, Black with maroon upholstery.
ENGINE: Cast iron block and head. Four-cylinder side-valve engine. Bore 73.5mm, stroke 87mm, 1476.5cc. Maximum bhp 41@4000rpm. SU horizontal carburettor (1¼in).
GEARBOX: Four-speed gearbox, bolted to rear engine plate. Synchromesh on second, third

and top gears. Column-mounted gearchange. Clutch: 7¼in single dry plate. Ratios: reverse

18.56:1, first 18.56:1, second 10.98:1, third 7.342:1, top 4.875:1.

REAR AXLE: Semi-floating hypoid bevel drive 4.875:1 8/39.

BRAKES: Lockheed hydraulic front and rear 8in diameter drums. Front: two leading shoes. Rear: one leading and one trailing shoe.

STEERING: Rack and pinion, 3 turns lock-to-lock.

TYRES: 5.25x15 bolt-on steel disc wheels later changed to 5.50x15, both with stud fixings.

SUSPENSION: Front: Independent with torsion bars and links. Rear: Semi-elliptic leaf springs. Hydraulic shock absorbers front and rear.

DIMENSIONS: **Length**: 13ft 9.5in (4.20m); **height**: 5ft 4in (1.63m); **width**: 5ft 5in (1.65m); **weight**: 22 cwt (1118kg); **turning circle**: 36ft (11m).

CAPACITIES: Fuel: 9 gallons (41 litres). Rear compartment: 35-60ft^3 (0.99-1.7m^3).

Morris Six Series MS

The Morris Six Series MS was showcased alongside the Morris Minor Series MM and the Morris Oxford Series MO at the 1948 London Motor Show at Earls Court. Unlike its counterparts, serious production of this model did not get under way until March 1949. The styling on the Morris Six mirrored that of the Morris Oxford rearwards of the windscreen. However, the frontal arrangement was strikingly different. The need to accommodate a taller and longer 2215cc six-cylinder overhead camshaft and valve engine meant that the engine bay was more elongated. A knock-on effect was the inclusion of an upright chrome radiator grille, more reminiscent of prewar cars, ahead of longer front wings which incorporated the headlights.

The early cars were dogged with structural and mechanical problems. In service, particularly in overseas markets where the terrain was more challenging, the nose heavy front end prompted severe weaknesses to be exposed at the base of the bulkhead. A fix needed to be devised and, after rigorous testing, additional strengthening by means of two triangular braces fitted from the inner wing to the bulkhead was fitted retrospectively. 1949 changes to improve handling included changing the lever arm dampers to telescopic

Lord Nuffield is reputed to have insisted on the upright radiator grille on the Morris Six MS.

shock absorbers at the rear. A year later a twin telescopic arrangement was adopted at the front.

The six-cylinder engine was also beset with problems. Poor cooling allied to a tendency to burn out exhaust valves after a relatively short time (10,000 to 15,000 miles) due to an inbuilt design fault did not bode well for sales. Stellited valves helped but were not adopted by the factory. To improve cooling issues a new revised cylinder head with improved waterways was introduced in 1952. The model was subject to other mechanical and styling changes during production, including revised rear lights in 1949, modified gear ratios, improved upholstery, the addition of a tinted rear mirror and a headlamp warning light during 1951/52. Standard equipment included an electric clock, an ammeter, and fuel and oil gauges.

Styling-wise the Morris Six MS provided the basis for models badged as Wolseley to be produced. The Wolseley 6/80 which was distinguished by its characteristic front grille, superior internal appointments including leather faced seats and interior wood trim and improved performance courtesy of twin SU

Gearchange diagram.

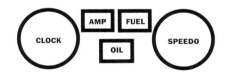

Instrument layout.

Morris Six, Oxford and Minor profiles: common parentage.

Only 11 Morris Six MS saloons were assigned to police duties in Britain. Wolseley 6/80 models proved more popular.

carburettors sold in large numbers, including a substantial quantity to the British Police. There was also a Wolseley 4/50 model which shared the same body but utilised a 1476cc four-cylinder version of the six-cylinder overhead camshaft and valve Wolseley engine. This was the same capacity as the Morris Oxford Series MO engine. It delivered an additional 10bhp but with little additional performance. The model was discontinued in 1952. Production of the Morris Six MS carried on until March 1953, whilst the more popular Wolseley 6/80 remained in production until October 1954.

PRODUCTION NUMBERS: Morris Six: 12,464.
PRICE ON INTRODUCTION: 1948 £607.
OPTIONAL EXTRAS: HMV radio £42 16s. 1d Heater. £13 8s 4d.
COLOURS ON INTRODUCTION: 1948 Romain Green, Platinum Grey, Black, Maroon, all with contrasting green, maroon, beige or brown trimming, and contrasting piping.
COLOURS THROUGHOUT PRODUCTION: Romain Green, Platinum Grey, Black, Maroon, Mist Green, Clarendon Grey, Birch Grey, Thames Blue and Empire Green.
ENGINE: 2.2-litre, six-cylinder overhead camshaft and valve engine. Bore 73.5mm (2.894in), stroke 87mm (3.425in), 2215cc. Maximum bhp 70 then 66. SU H4 (1½in) carburettor.
GEARBOX: Four-speed column-mounted gearlever. Synchromesh on second, third and fourth gears. Ratios: reverse 3.214, first 3.214, second 2.087, third 1.344, fourth 1.00.
REAR AXLE: Semi-floating hypoid type. Ratios 4:1:1 (10/41) then 4.55:1 (9/41)
BRAKES: Lockheed 10in diameter with two leading shoes in front. Drum brakes all round.
STEERING: Bishop cam and peg. Cam and roller steering box. 3.75 turns lock-to-lock.
TYRES: Large section Dunlop tyres 6.00x15in. Five-stud steel wheels.
SUSPENSION: Front: Independent by torsion bars and links in conjunction with hydraulic shock absorbers. Rear: Semi-elliptic springs and hydraulic double-acting shock absorbers front and rear.
DIMENSIONS: **Length**: 14ft 9in (4.496m); **height**: 5ft 3in (1.600m); **width**: 5ft 5in (1.651m); **weight**: 25cwt (1270kg); **turning circle**: 40ft (12m).
CAPACITIES: Fuel: 12 gallons (54.5 litres). Boot: 9.9ft^3.

Morris Oxford Series II

*High praise indeed for the new Morris
Oxford Series II saloon.*

The Morris Oxford Series II saloon
was introduced in May 1954 as
a replacement for the Morris
Oxford Series MO model. With
design input from Alec Issigonis,
it sported a restyled monocoque
body featuring a one-piece
curved windscreen, a revised
frontal arrangement – including
a bonnet that incorporated
an air intake scoop – and
distinctive 'Oxford' badging
positioned above a chrome
strip that extended along the
front wings and on to the
front doors. The generously
proportioned interior featured
a compact fascia featuring
two centrally positioned
circular instrumentation
clocks flanked by two open
glove boxes, a bench-type
front seat which, on the
driver's side, had a floor-
mounted handbrake lever,
and an oval cased steering column that
was slightly inclined to the right, so that three
people could be comfortably seated on the
front seat of right-
hand drive models.

Mechanically,
the Series II utilised
virtually the same
B series BMC
1498cc overhead
valve engine used
in the Austin A50
Cambridge model,
albeit with SU
rather than Zenith
carburettors. Though
a heavier car, the
Morris Oxford Series
II was still capable of
lively acceleration,
a top speed of
74mph, and a power
output of 50bhp at
4200rpm.

A Traveller model was introduced in October 1954. The front half of the Traveller was identical to the saloon. Rearward of the front doors, however, there was a steel frame clad with ash and aluminium infill panels. There was also an aluminium roof and aluminium rear door panelling. The bench-type front seat had a divided back which hinged forward to permit easy access on either side to the rear, and the rear seat back and squab also hinged forward to allow for additional storage space. The rear compartment was 52in (1.32m) wide and 63in (1.60m) long with the rear seat folded. An additional interesting design feature was

Instrument layout.

Gearchange layout.

Compact rear light unit and prominent Oxford badging.

the use of a protective rubber strip along the bottom of the rear wings.

The Series II Morris Oxford remained in production until October 1956 during which time relatively few modifications were made to the model specification. Changes in 1954 included revised bonnet stay arrangements and the fitting of a drip shield to the fuel pump, while in 1955 the steering column was lengthened and a modified gearchange and bracket added.

The Series II saloon was also assembled in India under licence by the Hindustan Motor Company and was marketed as the Hindustan Landmaster. Standard equipment included temperature and oil pressure gauges, ammeter, clock, heater, anti-dazzle driver's mirror, driver and passenger sun visors, leather seats, pile carpet, and front and rear over-riders. Traveller models had the seat arrangement described as above, along with rear windows with opening panels, and quarter rear bumpers instead of full width. Optional extras included a radio.

Morris Oxford Series II Travellers proved popular and boosted overall sales figures substantially. The Traveller is a very rare vehicle today.

PRODUCTION NUMBERS: 87,341 saloons. 72,816 Travellers.

PRICE: including purchase tax. Saloon: May 1954 £744, May 1956 £848, Traveller October 1954 £823, May 1956 £936.

COLOURS: Saloon: Black, Clarendon Grey, Sandy Beige, Empire Green, Smoke Blue for a limited period until replaced by Sandy Beige. Traveller: Clarendon Grey, Sandy Beige, Empire Green.

ENGINE: Four-cylinder, OHV, bore 73.025mm, stroke 89mm, 1489cc (90.88in³). Maximum bhp 50 at 4200rpm. SU H2 carburettor (1¼in).

GEARBOX: Four-speed, steering column gearchange, synchromesh on top three gears. Ratios on early cars: top 4.875, third 7.27, second 11.71, first 19.23, reverse 25.15.

REAR AXLE: Hypoid bevel, three-quarter floating, ratio 4.875:1

BRAKES: Lockheed, front and rear 9in drums.

STEERING: Rack and pinion.

TYRES: 5.50 x 15, spare wheel held vertically at side of luggage boot. Tyre size later changed to 5.60 x 15.

SUSPENSION: Front: Independent with torsion bars, wishbones, telescopic shock absorbers. Rear: Semi-elliptic leaf springs and telescopic shock absorbers.

DIMENSIONS: **Length**: saloon 14ft 3in (4.343m); **width**: 5ft 5in (1.65m); **height**: 5ft 3in (1.6m); **wheelbase**: 8ft 1in (2.46m); **track**: front 4ft 5.5in (1.36m), rear 4ft 5in (1.346m); **ground clearance**: 6.25in (15.9cm); **turning circle**: RH 35ft 6.5in (10.83m), LH 35ft 3in (10.74m); **weight**: 1ton 2cwt (1118kg). Traveller as saloon except **length**: 14ft 1in (4.29m); **weight**: 1ton 3cwt 2qtr (1195kg).

CAPACITIES: Fuel: Saloon 12 gallons (54 litres), Traveller 10 gallons (45 litres).

Saloon boot: 16ft³ (0.45m³), Traveller 65ft³ (1.828m³).

Morris Oxford Series III

The Series III Morris Oxford saloon and Traveller models introduced in October 1956 were a development from their predecessors in the Series II range. The facelift models featured a changed bonnet with fluted sides and lacked the air scoop of the previous model. Revised badging included a new bonnet motif with the Oxford designation prominently displayed beneath it, and the headlights now had hooded chrome surrounds. Squared-off rear wings housed round stop and tail lamps in an oval cluster, and chrome strips ran the length of the sides from atop the front wings to

which now had added protection courtesy of a sponge rubber covering, improved controls positioned within easier reach of the driver, and the inclusion of twin lidded glove boxes and a black dished steering wheel. Mechanically the Series III had an improved gear mechanism, and, from November 1957, the option of 'Manumatic' transmission, a two pedal semi-automatic system. In an improvement from the Series II, the engine received a welcome power boost courtesy of a higher compression ratio resulting in 55bhp from the 1498cc unit (previously 50bhp). In March 1958 a central, floor-mounted gearchange became available as an optional extra, and, to accommodate this, the front bench seat was modified to include a recess for the gearlever.

The Series III Traveller model mirrored

the rear, providing the demarcation for the optional duo-tone paint scheme. Prior to the introduction of the duo-tone paint option in February 1957 on Series III models the chrome strips appeared only on the top of the front and rear wings. A revised rear bumper was another distinguishing feature. Internal changes focussed on the fascia,

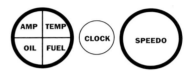

Instrument layout.

Gearchange layout on introduction.

most of the changes made to the internal specifications and frontal arrangement of the saloon models. The exception was the rear end styling which remained unchanged from that of the Series II version. The production run for the Traveller variant was short-lived. It was phased out in August 1957 and replaced by the Morris Oxford Series IV all-steel-bodied version.

Above: Modern variants. Hindustan Ambassador models, made in India.

Saloon production continued until March 1959 in Britain. However, the Series III Morris Oxford which was built in India and marketed there as the Hindustan Ambassador, enjoyed a long lease of life. Initially powered by the Morris engine and later by a derivative of the B series diesel engine option, these were eventually replaced by Isuzu-sourced engines in the late 1980s. As the Hindustan Ambassador, the vehicles were widely used as taxis and by senior police and other government agencies, and were a familiar sight throughout India where they remained in production until 2014.

Standard equipment for the Morris Oxford Series III included temperature and oil pressure gauges, ammeter, clock, heater, anti-dazzle driver's mirror, driver and passenger sun visor, leather seats, pile carpet, and front and rear over-riders. Optional extras included radio, windscreen washers, wheel rim embellishers, 'Manumatic' transmission, and duo-tone paint.

PRODUCTION NUMBERS: 52,235 saloons, 13,648 Travellers.
PRICE INCLUDING PURCHASE TAX: Saloon: 1956/57 £849, with 'Manumatic' £899, 1958 £885, with 'Manumatic' £935, 1959 £885. Traveller: 1956 £937, 1957 £975.
COLOURS: Saloon: Black, Clarendon Grey, Birch Grey, Sage Green, Dark Green, Turquoise, Pale Ivory. Duo-tone upper body colour first, Black/Birch Grey, Turquoise/Birch Grey, Dark Green/Island Green, Sage Green/Twilight Grey, Birch Grey/Red, Clarendon Grey/Steel Blue. Traveller: Single colour only option available. Clarendon Grey, Birch Grey, Dark Green.
ENGINE: Four-cylinder, OHV, bore 73.025mm, stroke 89.90mm, 1489cc (90.88in^3). Maximum bhp 55 at 4400rpm. SU H2 carburettor (1¼in).
GEARBOX: Four-speed, steering column gearchange, synchromesh on top three gears.

Ratios early cars: top 4.875, third 7.27, second 11.71, first 19.23, reverse 25.15.
REAR AXLE: Hypoid bevel, three-quarter floating, ratio 4.875:1.
BRAKES: Lockheed, front and rear 9in drums.
STEERING: Rack and pinion.
TYRES: Saloon, 5.50 x 15 on early cars 5.60 x 15 on later saloons and Travellers. Spare wheel held vertically at side of luggage boot in saloon and below the floor in the Traveller.
SUSPENSION: Front: Independent with torsion bars, wishbones, telescopic shock absorbers. Rear: Semi-elliptic leaf springs and telescopic shock absorbers.
DIMENSIONS: Length: saloon 14ft 3in (4.34m); **width:** 5ft 5in (1.65m); **height:** 5ft 3in (1.6m); **wheelbase:** 8ft 1in (2.46m); **track:** front 4ft 5.5in (1.36m), rear 4ft 5in (1.346m); **ground clearance:** 6.25in (16cm); **turning circle:** 33ft (10.06m); **weight:** saloon 22cwt (1118kg). Traveller as for saloon except for: **length:** 14ft 1in 4.29m; **weight:** 1159kg;

turning circle: R 33ft 3in (10.74m) L 33ft 6½in (10.84m).
CAPACITIES: Fuel: (saloon) 12 gallons (54 litres). Boot: 16ft^3 (0.453m^3). Fuel: (Traveller) 10 gallons (45.46 litres);. Rear compartment: 35-65ft^3 (1.84m^3).

Morris Oxford Series IV

The Morris Oxford Series IV designation was limited in its application, and only assigned to a new, all-steel-bodied Morris Oxford Traveller model. No Series IV Morris Oxford saloons were produced. Introduced in August 1957 to replace the Series III Traveller, the new four-door model had six side windows and a rear tailgate hinged at the top. The absence of wood framing and the inclusion of four doors set it apart from previous Traveller models in the Morris range. Other features included the use of a single fuel tank with fillers either side,

The all-steel-bodied Series IV Traveller represented a departure from previous ash-framed or ash-clad models.

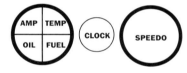

Instrument layout.

Gearchange layout.

and external side mouldings which helped delineate the respective areas for the optional duo-tone paint scheme. Production lasted until April 1960. Unlike the Series II and Series III Travellers the IV had a separate 'lower' floor area for the storage of the spare wheel and tools. A centrally positioned floor-mounted gearlever was an option from March 1958, and subsequently became standard. Standard equipment included oil pressure gauge, ammeter, clock, heater, anti-dazzle driver's mirror, driver and passenger sun visors, two glove boxes with lids, leather seats, centre arm rest in front bench seat, folding rear seat, opening front quarter lights, one-piece top-opening rear door for access to boot, and front and rear over-riders. Optional extras included radio, windscreen washers, duo-tone paint finish, and wheel rim embellishers.

COST INCLUDING PURCHASE TAX: 1957 £1003, 1958 £999, 1959/1960 £943.

COLOURS (1957): Single tone Black, Birch Grey, Clarendon Grey, Sage Green, Dark Green, Turquoise, Cream. Duo-tone upper body first, Black/Birch Grey, Black/Swiss Grey, Turquoise/Birch Grey, Turquoise/Swiss Grey, Sage Green/Twilight Grey, Dark Green/Island Green, Birch Grey/Red, Clarendon Grey/Steel Blue.

COLOURS (1959): Single tone, Black, Dark Grey, Dark Green, Light Green, Blue, Maroon. Duo-tone upper body first, Black/Dark Grey, Blue/Dark Grey, Dark Green/Light Green, Off White/Dark Green, Off White/Blue, Off White/Maroon.

ENGINE: Four-cylinder, OHV, bore 73.025mm, stroke 88.9mm, 1489cc (90.88in^3). Maximum bhp dependent on world sales area: 50 at 4800rpm with 7.2:1 compression or 55 with 8.3:1 compression. SU H2 carburettor (1¼in).

GEARBOX: Four-speed, steering column gearchange. Floor change option from March 1958 which later became standard. Synchromesh on top three gears. Ratios: top 4.875, third 7.266, second 11.715, first 19.23, reverse 25.15.

REAR AXLE: Hypoid bevel, three-quarter floating, ratio 4.875:1.

BRAKES: Lockheed, front and rear 9in drums.

STEERING: Rack and pinion.

TYRES: 5.50 x 15 and later 5.60 x 15. Spare wheel in separate compartment under boot floor accessible from outside the car.

SUSPENSION: Front: Independent with torsion bars with vernier adjustment, telescopic shock absorbers. Rear: Rubber-mounted semi-elliptic leaf springs and telescopic shock absorbers.

DIMENSIONS: Length: 14ft 2.5in (4.33m); **width:** 5ft 5in (1.65m); **height:** 5ft 3.5in (1.61m); **wheelbase:** 8ft 1in (2.46m); **track:** front 4ft 5.875in (1.37m), rear: 4ft 5.375in (1.36m); **ground clearance:** 6.25in (16cm); **turning circle:** LH 35.25ft (10.74m) RH 35.55ft (10.83m); **weight:** 1 ton 3cwt 3qtrs (1206kg).

CAPACITIES: Fuel: 11 gallons (50 litres). Boot: 26ft^3 (0.736m^3) or 50ft^3 (1.416m^3) with rear seat folded down.

The Morris Cowley 1200

Introduced in July 1954, the Morris Cowley 1200 four-door saloon was, in effect, a lower specification version of the Morris Oxford Series II saloon. Fitted with a 1200cc 'B' Series overhead valve engine capable of 42bhp, it differed not only in performance but in levels of internal and external trim. Leathercloth seat coverings, PVC-covered felt floor coverings, plain door cards, painted window frames with fixed quarter lights, an absence of chrome on the windscreen surround, over-riders on home market models, and chrome side flashes combined to set the Cowley apart. Cost savings, which amounted to £42 in 1954 compared to the Oxford Series II, extended to there being only one sun visor, no chrome horn ring on the steering wheel, less instrumentation and brightwork, and to the heater being non-standard. 8in brake drums were fitted on introduction, though they were increased in size to 9in within three months. Standard equipment included an oil pressure gauge, ammeter and a driver's sun visor. Optional extras on home market models included a heater, radio and over-riders. The Cowley 1200 remained in production until October 1956 when it was replaced by the Cowley 1500 saloon. Only saloon models of the Cowley 1200 were produced.

PRODUCTION NUMBERS: 17,413.

COST ON INTRODUCTION: 1954 £702, 1956 £799.

COLOURS: Black, Clarendon Grey, Sandy Beige, Empire Green, Smoke Blue for a limited time until replaced by Sandy Beige.

ENGINE: Four-cylinder, OHV, bore 65.48mm, stroke 89.90mm, 1200cc (73.17in^3). Maximum bhp 42 at 4500rpm. SU H2 carburettor (1¼in).

GEARBOX: Four-speed, steering column gearchange, synchromesh on top three gears. Ratios: top 5.125, third 7.638, second 12.315, first 20.220, reverse 26.44.

The Cowley 1200 was only produced as a basic four-door saloon.

REAR AXLE: Hypoid bevel, three-quarter floating, ratio 5.125:1 (8/41).
BRAKES: Lockheed, front and rear 8in drums initially then 9in.
STEERING: Rack and pinion.
TYRES: 5.60 x 15, spare wheel held vertically at side of luggage boot.
SUSPENSION: Front: Independent with torsion bars, wishbones, telescopic shock absorbers. Rear: Semi-elliptic leaf springs and telescopic shock absorbers.

Instrument layout.

Gearchange layout.

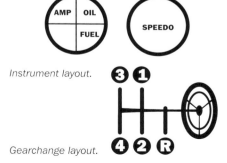

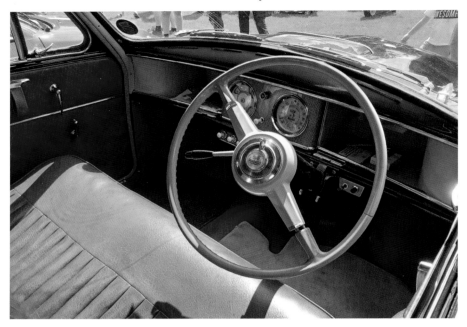

DIMENSIONS: **Length**: 14ft 1in (4.29m); **width**: 5ft 5in (1.65m), **height** 5ft 3in (1.6m); **wheelbase**: 8ft 1in (2.46m); **track**: front 4ft 5.5in (1.36m), rear 4ft 5in (1.346m); **ground clearance**: 6.75in (17.1cm); **turning circle**: LH 35ft 3in (10.74m), RH 35ft 6.25in (10.83m); **weight**: 1ton 2cwt (1118kg). **CAPACITIES**: Fuel: 12 gallons (54 litres). Boot: 16ft³ (0.45m³).

Morris Cowley 1500

Introduced in 1956, the Morris Cowley 1500 was advertised as being glamorous, and with many new features, including new colours, new contours and more power. With styling based on the Morris Oxford Series III, and utilising the 1498cc overhead valve engine used in the Oxford, the new Cowley represented an improvement over the previous 1200 model. Compared with the Oxford Series III, however, it had a more basic specification, with standard equipment limited to an oil pressure gauge, ammeter, driver's sun visor, a single horn and leathercloth upholstery. Absent from the

specification were a heater, a temperature gauge, passenger sun visor and the option of duo-tone paint. Unlike the Morris Oxford Series III it did not have hooded headlamp surrounds, vertical grille embellishers, brightwork surrounds to the windows and screens or side panel chrome mouldings. Windscreen washers, a radio and a heater were available as optional extras. Despite the restyling and the optimistic advertising, the Cowley 1500, which, incidentally, was the last Morris to carry that name, did not sell well. It was discontinued in March 1959.

PRODUCTION NUMBERS: 4632.
COST ON INTRODUCTION: 1956 £799.
COLOURS: Black, Birch Grey, Clarendon Grey, Sage Green, Dark Green, Turquoise, Cream.
ENGINE: Four-cylinder, OHV, bore 73.025mm, stroke 88.9mm, 1489cc (90.88in³). Maximum 55bhp at 4400rpm. SU H2 carburettor (1¼in).
GEARBOX: Four-speed, steering column gearchange, later central floor change, synchromesh on top three gears. Ratios top 4.875, third 7.266, second 11.715, first 19.23, reverse 25.15.

Fewer than 5000 Cowley 1500 models were sold.

Morris ceased to use the Cowley name when Cowley 1500 production came to an end.

REAR AXLE: Hypoid bevel, three-quarter floating, ratio 4.875:1(8/39).
BRAKES: Lockheed, front and rear 9in drums.
STEERING: Rack and pinion. 3.125 turns lock-to-lock.
TYRES: 5.60 x15.
SUSPENSION: Front: Independent with torsion bars, wishbones, telescopic shock absorbers. Rear: Semi-elliptic leaf springs and telescopic shock absorbers.

DIMENSIONS: **Length**: 14ft 1in (4.29m); **width**: 5ft 5in (1.65m); **height**: 5ft 3in (1.6m); **wheelbase**: 8ft 1in (2.46m); **track**: front 4ft 5.5in (1.36m), rear 4ft 5in (1.346m); **ground clearance**: 6.25in (15.9cm); **turning circle**: LH 35ft 3in (10.74m) RH 35ft 6.6in (10.83m); **weight**: 1ton 1cwt 10lb (1071kg),
CAPACITIES: Fuel: saloon 12 gallons (54 litres). Boot: 16ft^3 (0.45m^3).

Left-hand drive Cowley 1500 fascia.

Morris Isis Series I

Introduced in July 1955, the Morris Isis was an attempt to reintroduce a six-cylinder engine car into the Morris range following the demise of the Morris Six MS in 1953. In terms of body design, it was essentially an elongated version of the Morris Oxford Series II, with a larger frontal arrangement with additional bracing to support and accommodate the larger, heavier 2639cc overhead valve power unit. The Isis was available in standard and deluxe specification, and as a four-door saloon and a Traveller estate. Like the Morris Oxford Series II Traveller the steel framed aluminium-clad rear body was enhanced by wooden framing to the sides and rear doors. Other Isis features included Bishop Cam steering mounted ahead of the front suspension, and, from early 1956, the option of Borg-Warner overdrive. Late Series 1 models had a mesh grille, which was introduced in June 1956, and coloured piping on the seats. Standard equipment included temperature and oil pressure gauges, an ammeter, a full width parcel shelf, pile carpets, and leathercloth-covered seats. Deluxe models boasted a heater, additional instrumentation in the

No mistaking this Isis!

Instrument layout.

Gearchange layout.

shape of a clock, twin horns, leather seats with a centre armrest in the rear seat, opening quarter-lights in the front doors, as well as chrome over-riders. Traveller model specifications mirrored that of the deluxe saloons except for folding rear seats, a hinged divided front seatback to facilitate access to the rear, a third row of 'occasional' seats in the back, split rear bumpers without over-riders, and a smaller fuel tank. The Isis Series I stayed in production until October 1956 by which time a combined total of 8541 saloons and Travellers had been produced.

PRODUCTION NUMBERS: 6691 saloons 1850 Travellers.

COST ON INTRODUCTION: 1954 standard saloon £801, deluxe saloon £844, 1955 Traveller £957.

COLOURS: Black (not Traveller), Clarendon Grey, Sandy Beige, Empire Green.

ENGINE: Six-cylinder, OHV, bore 79.375mm, stroke 88.9mm, 2639cc (161in^3). Maximum bhp 86 at 4250rpm. SU H4 carburettor (1½in).

GEARBOX: Four-speed, steering column gearchange, synchromesh on top three gears. Ratios: top 4.1, third 5.88, second 8.45, first 13.59, reverse 18.42, with optional overdrive, o/d top 2.87, o/d third 4.12, o/d second 5.91, first 13.59.

REAR AXLE: Hypoid bevel, three-quarter floating, ratio 4.1:1 with or without overdrive.

BRAKES: Lockheed, front and rear, initially 10in then 11in drums.

STEERING: Bishop cam and lever. 3.5 turns lock-to-lock.

C Series 2639cc engine.

TYRES: Standard saloon 6.40 x 15, deluxe saloon and Traveller estate 6.00 x 15.

SUSPENSION: Front: Independent with torsion bars and telescopic shock absorbers. Rear: Semi-elliptic leaf springs and telescopic shock absorbers.

DIMENSIONS: **Length**: saloon 14ft 10in (4.52m); **width**: 5ft 5in (1.65m); **height**: saloon 5ft 3.75in (1.62m); **wheelbase**: 8ft 11.5in (2.73m); **track**: front 4ft 5.5in (1.36m), rear 4ft 5in (1.346m); **ground clearance**: 7in (18cm); **turning circle**: LH 36ft 9in (11.15m) RH 37ft 6.5in (11.43m); **weight**: saloon 1ton 5.75cwt (1308kg).

Traveller as saloon except for **length**: 14ft 8.69in (4.487m); **height**: 5ft 3.94in (1.623m); **weight**: 1ton 5.75cwt (1308kg).

CAPACITIES: Fuel: saloon 12 gallons

(54 litres), Traveller 10 gallons (45 litres). Boot: saloon 16ft³ (0.45m³), Traveller with seats folded 65ft³ (1.840m³), with seats upright 35ft³ (0.99m³).

Morris Isis Series II

Introduced in October 1956 the Morris Isis Series II model range included a restyled four-door saloon model along with an updated version of the Traveller estate. On the saloon the body shape was altered to include a fluted bonnet, 'squared-up' rear wings, new rear lamp units, and chrome strips on the tops of front and rear wings and on the side panels from April 1957 to delineate for the later duo-tone paint options. This later duo-tone delineation was not the same as on the Oxford Series III as the Isis bonnet was the lower colour, the Oxford was the top. Mechanical changes included improved power output from the 2.6-litre, six-cylinder OHV engine courtesy of raised compression ratio from 7.3 to 8.2 and an increase to 90bhp. The gearchange was moved from the steering column to the floor with an innovative positioning on the right-hand side of the driver's seat, just ahead of the handbrake. Borg-Warner automatic transmission and Borg-Warner overdrive were also available as optional extras. Internally, a new fascia panel with well grouped controls featured twin lidded glove boxes. On deluxe models duo-tone upholstery with leather on wearing surfaces and nylon leathercloth elsewhere was a new feature. Deluxe specification also included wheel rim embellishers, twin horns, heater, central rear seat arm rest, windscreen washers, opening front quarter lights, and over-riders. Other optional extras included a radio and, for saloon models only, a range of duo-tone paint colours which were available for an additional £15. Internal Traveller appointments mirrored those of the deluxe saloon, with similar seating arrangements to the Series I version, including the occasional seats in the back which increased the carrying capacity to eight passengers.

The Series II Traveller was phased out in October 1957. The saloon followed in April 1958. Combined production of saloon and Traveller models totalled 3614.

PRICE ON INTRODUCTION: October 1956.

The duo-tone paint scheme on Isis models differed from that used on Oxford Series III models.

The dashboard layout on Series II models featured two lidded glove boxes.

Instrument layout.

Gearchange layout.

Elaborate Isis Series II bonnet badge.

Handbrake and gear lever position on right-hand drive models.

Isis saloon standard £911, Isis saloon deluxe £961, Isis Traveller £1089, Borg-Warner overdrive £63, Borg-Warner automatic transmission £172.

COLOURS: Single tone Black, Birch Grey, Clarendon Grey, Sage Green, Dark Green, Turquoise, Cream. Duo-tone upper body first, Black/Swiss Grey, Turquoise/Swiss Grey, Sage Green/Twilight Grey, Dark Green/Island Green, Birch Grey/Red, Clarendon Grey/Steel Blue, Birch Grey/Red. Note two-tone upholstery was always pale beige leather with, according to exterior colour, black, red or green nylon trim. Single tone upholstery was either grey, red or green depending on exterior body colour(s). Traveller. Duo-tone colours not an option. Monotone colours limited to Dark Green, Clarendon Grey, Birch Grey.

ENGINE: Six-cylinder, OHV, bore 79.375mm, stroke 88.9mm, 2639cc (161in³), maximum bhp 90 at 4250rpm. SU H4 carburettor (1½in).

GEARBOX: Four-speed, floor-mounted gearchange by side of driver's seat, synchromesh on top three gears, ratios, top 4.1, third 5.88, second 8.45, first 13.59, reverse 18.4, with optional overdrive, o/d top

2.87, third 4.11, second 5.91, first 13.59, reverse 18.42.

REAR AXLE: Hypoid bevel, three-quarter floating, ratio 4.1 (10/41) with or without overdrive.

BRAKES: Lockheed, front and rear 11in drums.

STEERING: Bishop cam and lever.

TYRES: Standard saloon 6.40 x 15, deluxe saloon and Traveller estate 6.00 x 15.

SUSPENSION: Front: Independent with torsion bars with vernier adjustment, wishbones and telescopic shock absorbers. Rear: Semi-elliptic leaf springs and telescopic shock absorbers.

DIMENSIONS: Length: saloon 14ft 10in (4.52m); **width**: 5ft 5in (1.65m); **height**: saloon 5ft 3.75in (1.62m); **wheelbase**: 8ft

11.5in (2.73m); **track**: front 4ft 5.5in
(1.36m), rear 4ft 5in (1.346m); **ground
clearance**: 7in (18cm); **turning circle**:
LH 36ft 9in (11.15m) RH 37ft 6.5in
(11.43), Traveller as saloon except
length: 14ft 8.69in (4.487m); **height**:
5ft 3.94in (1.623m); **weight**: saloons
1ton 6cwt 2qtr 4lb (1349kg), Traveller 1
ton 7cwt 1qtr (1410kg)
CAPACITIES: Fuel: Saloons 12 gallons
(54 litres), Traveller 10 gallons (45
litres). Boot: Saloons 16ft³ (0.453m³),
Traveller with rear seats folded down
65ft³ (1.828m³).

Morris Mini Minor

The Morris Mini Minor was introduced in August 1959 alongside its Austin counterpart the Austin Se7en (later known as the Austin Mini). Designed by Alec Issigonis, who had returned to BMC following a brief interlude when he worked for Alvis Motors, the ADO 15 project, as it had been named, was destined to be yet another masterpiece in the Issigonis design portfolio following the success of the postwar Morris Minor. His brief, set against the backdrop of the Suez crisis when supplies of oil were cut off and fuel rationing was introduced in Britain, was to produce a small, compact, fuel efficient car capable of carrying four people. The result was an innovative vehicle just 10ft long, and featuring many new design concepts. In order to maximise interior space, the decision was taken to produce a front-wheel drive car thus eliminating the need for a transmission tunnel running through the centre of the vehicle to accommodate a propshaft. By mounting the engine transversely and accommodating the gearbox underneath the engine in the sump, a more compact front end arrangement was achieved. Other features, such as 10in wheels, minimised rear wheelarch intrusion, and, with storage space inside the car maximised using a full width front parcel shelf, space under the rear seats and door bins, a smaller boot was feasible. A novel feature was a hinged rear number plate which hung down when the boot lid was left open thus providing an option to increase the carrying capacity. Other innovations included the use of sub frames for the engine and suspension,

Sectioned Mini pictured at the British Motor Museum.

1959 (left) and 1961 Morris Mini Minors; both in 'as new' condition.

and, instead of conventional steel springs, an Alex Moulton-designed rubber cone suspension system comprising inner and outer cones with rubber inserted between them, which compressed when the car ran over uneven surfaces. Both Morris and Austin models used an 848cc short stroke version of the BMC A series engine in conjunction with a four-speed gearbox with floor gearchange and synchromesh on the upper three gears. The Morris Mini Minor and the Austin Se7en models were well received when launched, though there were early teething problems, mostly to do with the ingress of water into the floor area of the passenger compartment, and on to the

plug leads and ignition components in the engine bay. The latter was rectified by fitting a plastic cover over the plug leads.

A hinged number plate allowed for goods to be transported with the boot open.

Functional interior ... as stipulated by Alec Issigonis.

Basic and deluxe models of the Morris Mini Minor were available from the outset. Deluxe models benefitted from having additional brightwork in the form of bright metallised plastic beading on the wheelarches and along the lower body sills, bright inserts in the windscreen and rear screen surrounds, chromium plated fuel filler cap and rear number plate lamp, and chromium plate wheel embellishers. In addition, an adjustable passenger seat, foam rubber seat cushions, twin sun visors, a heater, windscreen washers, duo-tone upholstery, ashtrays and outward hinging rear quarter windows were added to the specification.

The model range was increased in 1960 when a quarter-ton van version was introduced. In September of the same year a Morris Mini Traveller was added, and this was followed in March 1961 by a pick-up model. All these models had a 4in longer wheelbase than the saloons. There was a proliferation of designations for both Morris and Austin versions in the early 1960s and other marques introduced, including Wolseley Hornet and Riley Elf versions 1961. Morris Mini Minors gained the designation 'Super' saloons in June 1961, but within a year 'deluxe' and 'super' saloon were replaced by 'Super Deluxe' versions. Super Deluxe models benefitted from the following additional items: three clock dash binnacle, rubber boot mat, heater, interior light, rear ashtrays, over-riders and corner bars, full chrome wheel trims and sill finishers.

In September 1961 the first of the Morris Mini Cooper models was announced. Featuring a 997cc engine capable of 55bhp it had twin 1¼in carburettors, a three-branch exhaust system, front disc brakes, a grille featuring seven horizontal bars, special badging and other refinements. It became an instant success within the motorsport fraternity.

Further changes took place in 1964 when the Super Deluxe designation changed to Deluxe. This coincided with the introduction of Hydrolastic suspension to saloon models. It was not used on vans, pick-ups or Traveller models. The Hydrolastic suspension system operated using cylinders containing a fluid which was compressed when the car hit a bump absorbing the impact and causing the fluid to flow via the interconnected front and rear pipework to the rear of the car ready for the rear wheels to encounter the bump.

Morris Mini Minor Traveller. Early Austin variants were designated the Austin Seven Countryman.

53

Automatic transmission became available as an option in 1965. By this time, it was estimated that 5600 'Minis' of all types were being built each week, and, in February 1965 the millionth Mini was built at Longbridge. Mk I versions of the Morris Mini Minor continued in production until October 1967 when further upgrades resulted in the Mk II models being announced.

Standard equipment for the 1962 Basic saloon models included large front door bins, cubby box with ashtray either side of rear seat, cloth trimmed seats, Deluxe added heater, windscreen washers, passenger sun visor, opening rear quarter lights, vinyl treated fabric trim, vinyl covered dashboard, door kick plates, bumper over-riders, wheel trims and bright finish for sills and windows and chrome plated petrol cap and rear number plate surround, Super specification featured water temperature and oil pressure gauges, roof-mounted interior light, chromed lever-type interior door handles instead of pull strings, over riders with 'nudge bars,' stainless steel window surrounds and sill finishers, duo-tone paint scheme with roof in white or black and front grille with vertical bars in addition to the horizontal bars of the Basic and Deluxe. Optional equipment included

Other changes introduced at the same time included changes to the gearbox, a new clutch, improved front brakes, and the introduction of a combined ignition key and starter switch to replace the floor-mounted starter button.

radio, wing mirrors (standard on Traveller). For the 1962 Super Deluxe the interior door handles were replaced by the pull cord type of door opener, the front ashtrays gained lids and the front grille was changed.

Basic and Deluxe Mini instruments (left), Super and Mini Cooper dashboard layout (below).

PRODUCTION NUMBERS: 510,000 approximately.

PRICE: 1959. Basic saloon £497, Deluxe £537, 1962 prices Basic £496, Deluxe £535, Super £561, Traveller estate £627, all-steel estate £608.

COLOURS (1959): Cherry Red, Clipper Blue, Old English White.

ENGINE: Four-cylinder, OHV, bore 62.94mm, stroke 68.26mm, 848cc (51.8in^3), maximum bhp 34. SU HS2 carburettor.

GEARBOX: Four-speed, floor-mounted gearchange, synchromesh on top three gears. Ratios: top 3.765, third 5.316, second 8.178, first 13.659, reverse 13.659. Front-wheel drive with helical spur gears and open drive shafts with universal joints, final drive ratio 3.765:1

BRAKES: Lockheed front and rear 7in drums with handbrake between the front seats.

STEERING: Rack and pinion

TYRES: 5.20 x 10.

SUSPENSION: Front: Independent wishbone. Rear: Independent trailing arms, with Moulton rubber cone springs and Armstrong telescopic shock absorbers front and rear.

Gearchange layout.

DIMENSIONS: **Length**: saloon, 10ft 0.25in (3.05m), **width**: 4ft 7.5in (1.41m), **height**: 4ft 5in (1.346m), **wheelbase**: 6ft 8in (2.03m), **track**: front 3ft 11.325in (1.203m), rear 3ft 9.875in (1.165m), **ground clearance**: 6.125in (1.56cm), **turning circle**: 31ft 7in (9.63m), estate as saloon except **length**: 10ft 9.9in (2.14m), **height** :4ft 5.5in (1.36m), **wheelbase**: 7ft 0.25in (2.14m); **unladen weight**: saloon 12cwt 1qtr 8lb (626.38kg). **CAPACITIES**: Fuel: 5.5 gallons (25 litres). Boot: 6ft^3 (1.7m^3), estate 18.5ft^3 (0.52m^3) or 35.5ft^3 (1.01m^3) with rear seat folded down.

Morris Mini Mark II

In October 1967 the Mini range was slightly restyled and given a mechanical upgrade. Externally the main differences were a revised front grille which was larger with a changed profile, a larger rear window and bigger rear light with a more angular shape. Super Deluxe models had a changed fascia panel with a three-instrument arrangement like that used in the Mini Cooper. More significantly, an additional engine choice was now available to complement the well tried and tested 848cc. A 998cc engine

with remote control gearchange which was already in use in the Wolseley Hornet and Riley Elf versions was now made available. Additional changes included revisions to the rack and pinion steering, a marked reduction in the turning circle, improved braking and a new indicator stalk which incorporated headlamp flasher and dip switch operation. AP automatic transmission was made available as an option for use with both engines. Further improvements followed in 1968 when an all synchromesh transmission was phased in on manual models and internal door handles replaced the original pull cords.

The car range now comprised Morris 850, 850 Super Deluxe. 1000 Super Deluxe and Traveller models. There were Austin versions of all the above and 850 and 1000 vans and pick-ups. The Traveller Estate had the revised Mk II frontal arrangement but retained the rear lights, etc used on the Mk I models. It was, however, only offered with the 998cc engine. Optional extras included seatbelts, automatic transmission, reclining front seats, fresh air heater and a heated rear window. The Mk II models remained in production until 1969 when, as part of a rationalisation

Mk II models are easily distinguished by larger and more angular rear light clusters, and a larger rear screen.

Mk II Traveller without wooden battens.

programme undertaken by British Leyland Motor Corporation following the takeover of BMC in 1968, both Austin and Morris names were dropped from the Mini designation. From that point on 'Mini' became the recognised marque name for the models, even though Austin-Morris remained a division within the newly established British Leyland.

Manual gearchange layout.

PRODUCTION NUMBERS: 206,000 approximately.

PRICE: 1968. Morris Mini Mk II Saloon (Basic) £561, Morris Mini Mk II (848cc) Super De-luxe Saloon £609, Morris Mini Mk II (998cc) Super De-luxe Saloon £634, Morris Mini Mk II Traveller (excluding wooden battens) £672, Morris Mini Mk II Traveller (including wooden battens) £692

COLOURS (1968): Snowberry White, Tartan Red, Mineral Blue, Cumulus Grey, Porcelain Green, El Paso Beige.

R
N
1
2
3
4
D

Automatic gearchange layout.

ENGINE: Four-cylinder, OHV, 850, bore 62.94mm, stroke 68.26mm, 848cc ($51.8in^3$), maximum bhp 34. SU HS2 carburettor. 1000, bore 64.58mm, stroke 76.2mm, 998cc ($60.89in^3$), maximum bhp 38 at 5250rpm. SU HS4 carburettor. Note the 998cc engine was derived from the 1098cc engine used in the Morris 1100 models. It was not developed from the 848cc engine.

GEARBOX: Four-speed, floor-mounted gearchange, synchromesh on top three gears. Ratios: top 3.44, third 4.86, second 7.47, first 12.48 reverse 12.48. Front-wheel drive with helical spur gears and open drive shafts with universal joints, final drive ratio 3.44:1. Note 848cc engine retained the original Mark I ratios. All synchromesh gearbox introduced (1968).

BRAKES/STEERING/TYRES: As Mini Mark I.

SUSPENSION: Initially, front independent wishbone, rear trailing arms with interconnected front and rear Hydrolastic displacers then from 1969 reverted to rubber cone type.

DIMENSIONS: As Mini Mark I except turning circle now 28ft 6in (8.6m).

Morris Mini Cooper and Cooper S

Introduced in September 1961, the Mini Cooper Saloon used the A series engine which had a longer stroke and reduced bore and a capacity of 997cc. Differences over the other models in the range included twin carburettors, front disc brakes, remote control gearchange, and a different front grille. One of the most striking features was the two-tone paint scheme, with the roof being painted in either black or white according to the main body colour. In 1963 an additional Cooper model, the S, was introduced. This retained the same stroke as the original standard cars but had an enlarged bore producing a 1071cc engine. Other changes from the 997cc Cooper included larger, power assisted discs brakes. It also had wider front and rear track and had radial instead of cross-ply tyres as standard. At the beginning of 1964 a 998cc engine that had been introduced with the

Riley Elf and Wolseley Hornet Mark II models replaced the original 997cc Cooper unit. This new engine had a shorter stroke and wider bore. The Cooper version was once again fitted with twin carburettors. In April 1964 the 1071cc Cooper S was replaced by two new models with 970cc and 1275cc engines. The 1275cc engine was destined to become the sole Mini Cooper engine. The last of the original Mini Cooper series of cars, the 1275 S, was discontinued in 1971. After this the Mini Clubman 1275 GT, which had been introduced in 1969, took over the role as the sole performance model until all Clubman models were phased out with the introduction of the Metro in 1980. The Mini Cooper name would, however, reappear in 1990 as part of a range of special edition models, and it marked the return of the 1275cc engine to the Mini. The Cooper name then disappeared again when all Minis were discontinued in 2000.

PRODUCTION NUMBERS: Cooper 997cc 12,465, 998cc Mark I 21,627, Mark II 7228.

963 Mini Cooper S 970cc models were built.

Cooper S 1071cc 1896, 970cc 963, 1275cc Mark I 7824, Mark II 3642, Mark III 19,511 (note Mark III models were not produced as separate Austin and Morris models).

Details of Morris Cooper models with differences from standard 848cc Mini as follows: 997 model: September 1961 to 1964. Instruments as Super model, 16-blade

Mk II Morris Mini Cooper and Morris Mini Cooper S models.

The motorsport potential of the Mini Cooper models was promoted in period brochures.

cooling fan from late 1961. Price. Cooper saloon 1961 £697

ENGINE: Bore 62.43mm, stroke 81.28mm, 997cc (60.86in^3), maximum bhp 55 at 6000rpm, two SU HS2 carburettors.
GEARBOX: Floor-mounted remote control gearchange lever. Ratios: top 3.765, third 5.11, second 7.21, first 12.05, reverse 12.05. Final drive ratio 3.765 with the option of 3.44:1 (see 1071 model).
BRAKES: Front 7in discs, rear 7in drums.

DIMENSIONS: Track: front 3ft 11.75in (1.213m); **weight**: 12cwt 2qtr (636kg).

998 model: January 1964 to 1969. Note Mark II model introduced in October 1967 had new rear lights, enlarged rear window and revised shape front grille. Price 1964 £590.

ENGINE: Bore 64.6mm, stroke 76.2mm, 998cc (60.86in^3), maximum bhp 55 at 5800rpm. Two SU HS2 carburettors.
GEARBOX: As 997cc model but with new type

diaphragm clutch from September 1964 and all synchromesh gearbox from late 1968.
TYRES: 145 x 10 radial ply.
SUSPENSION: Early cars rubber cone type, then from September 1964, front independent wishbone, rear trailing arms with interconnected Hydrolastic displacers front and rear.
DIMENSIONS: As 997cc model.

1071 S: April 1963 to September 1964. Equipment as Mini Cooper, except ventilated wheels, additional 5.5-gallon fuel tank, oil cooler, sumpguard. Price 1963 £695.

ENGINE: Bore 70.64mm, stroke 68.26mm, 1071cc (65.3in^3), maximum bhp 70 at 6000rpm. Two SU HS2 carburettors.
GEARBOX: Floor-mounted remote control gearlever, standard ratios as Cooper with 3.765 final drive, with optional 3.44 final drive, top 3.44, third 4.66, second 6.59, first 11.0. A close ratio gearbox was also available.
BRAKES: Front 7.5in discs, rear 7in drums, power assisted.
DIMENSIONS: **Track**: front 4ft 0.4in (1.229m), rear 3ft 10.9in (1.191m); **weight**: 12cwt 2qtr 10lb (640kg).

970 S: April 1964 to January 1965. Price 1964 £693.

ENGINE: Bore 70.64mm, stroke 61.91mm, 970cc (59.21in^3), maximum bhp 65 at 6500rpm. Two SU HS2 carburettors.
SUSPENSION: Rubber cone initially then Hydrolastic from September 1964.

1275 S: April 1964 to July 1971. Twin fuel tanks became standard in 1966, along with modifications to the suspension. Note Mark II model introduced in October 1967 had new rear lights, enlarged rear window and revised shape front grille. The Mark III introduced in March 1970 featured concealed door hinges and wind-up windows, but was no longer offered with two-tone paint scheme. Price 1964 £778.

Mini Cooper Mk II 1968 £694. Mini Cooper 'S' Mark II 1968 £921

ENGINE: Bore 70.64mm, stroke 81.33mm, 1275cc (77.8in^3), maximum 76bhp at 5800rpm. Two SU HS2 carburettors.
GEARBOX: Four-speed, synchromesh on top three gears. Ratios: as 1071 S, all synchromesh gearbox from 1968.
DIMENSIONS: **Track**: front 3ft 11.53in (1.207m), rear 3ft 10.31in (1.176m); **weight**: 13cwt 2qtr 23lb (698kg).
CAPACITIES (FROM 1966): Fuel: 11 gallons (50 litres). Boot: 4ft^3 (0.11m^3).

Morris Mini Moke

The Mini Moke became available in August 1964 as a general multi-purpose vehicle. Austin and Morris badged versions were available from the outset. Originally the Moke was developed with a military use in mind but the lack of take up from the armed services resulted in it being put into general production. It was built at both the Longbridge and Cowley assembly plants. Ironically, customs and excise designated the Mini Moke as a passenger car rather than a commercial vehicle due to its lack of load carrying space.

Mechanically, the Mini Moke was similar to the standard 848cc Mini models. The engine was slightly de-tuned and employed a different type of ignition distributor (Lucas 25D4) which was more tolerant of low-grade fuel. The suspension was the same as that used on the Mini van, pick-up and Traveller models which used the rubber cone system. Other mechanical components, including the gearbox and braking system, mirrored that of the 848cc Mini. Regarding the rest of the specification it is probably best described as functional. The fully rust proofed open body was of unitary construction. It had a folding detachable windscreen, basic seating with a detachable driver's seat and a vinyl treated tilt cover. The tubular supports for the tilt could be removed leaving a totally open vehicle.

The 'Moke' received considerable publicity following its use in the contemporary television programme *The Prisoner*. Several aftermarket kits, which were approved by BMC, provided additional weather protection. Barton Motor Co Ltd in Plymouth, England produced a range of glassfibre panels which allowed for an all enclosed body with doors and rear quarter side windows to be fitted.

The Mini Moke remained in production in

Austin and Morris versions of the Mini Moke were produced (see text). Ultimately, though, the Moke was more suited to the beach than the military.

Speedometer with four warning lights and fuel gauge (same as the 1098cc Morris Minor).

Compact transversely-mounted 848cc engine shoehorned into 18 inches.

the UK until October 1968. Production was then moved to Australia where Morris Mini Mokes and later Leyland Mokes continued to be built until 1981. Final production models were built in Portugal.

PRODUCTION NUMBERS: 14,518.
PRICE: (vehicle with driver's seat only) October 1964 £406, October 1967 £413 1968 £462.
OPTIONAL EXTRAS: Passenger seat with grab handle, rear seats with grab handles, sumpguard, Weathermaster tyres, laminated screen and windscreen washer.
ENGINE: Four-cylinder OHV 848cc, bore 62.9mm, stroke 68.26 mm 34bhp at 5500rpm. SU HS2 carburettor.
GEARBOX. Four-speed gearbox, central floor change, synchromesh on top three gears. Ratios: top 1.00, third 1.412, second 2.172, first 3.628, reverse 3.628. Front-wheel drive with helical spur gears and open drive shafts with universal joints.

BRAKES: Lockheed front and rear 7in drums.
STEERING: Rack and pinion.
SUSPENSION: Moulton rubber cone spring suspension. Armstrong telescopic shock absorbers front and rear.
DIMENSIONS: **Length**: 10ft; **height**: (hood to ground) (4ft 8in), screen to ground (4ft 3¾in); **width**: (4ft 3½in; **ground clearance**: 6⅛in.
CAPACITIES: Fuel: 5.5 gallons (25 litres).

Morris 1100 Mark I

Sir Alec Issigonis was responsible for the design of the Morris 1100, codenamed ADO16. He was ably assisted by Charles Griffin, BMC Chief engineer, and a talented team of engineers who helped develop some innovative ideas for the new car. Body design was by the Italian company Pininfarina, and the result was a stylish, compact yet roomy vehicle. Though development was ongoing in 1959, it was not until August 1962 that ADO16 was launched as the Morris 1100. Key features of the car included the front-wheel drive configuration using a transversely mounted 1098cc version of the A series engine with a four-speed gearbox, 12in wheels and Hydrolastic suspension. The Hydrolastic suspension developed by Alex Moulton was an advanced system that employed intercoupled units which automatically controlled fluid displacement, thus preserving the balance of the car while providing a controlled smooth ride. Its use transformed the comfort and ride quality, and was widely publicised by the marketing department.

Alec Issigonis and Charles Griffen led the design team working on the Morris 1100.

At launch the Morris 1100 was available as a four-door saloon in either Basic or Deluxe specification. Interestingly, although some of the development work occurred in the design offices at Austin's Longbridge plant, almost a year elapsed before the equivalent Austin 1100 models became available, and it was a further two years before Wolseley and Riley versions went on sale. An addition to the range occurred in March 1966 when a two-door estate model was introduced. A top-hinged rear tailgate provided easy access to a sizeable rear load area when the rear seat was folded forward. When reclining front

Morris 1100 Mk I Deluxe four-door saloon. Very few early Basic four-door saloons were sold in Britain.

seats were specified as an optional extra the vehicle was capable of use with a 6ft 6in long sleeping compartment. In 1965 an AP four-speed automatic transmission option became available, and a heater became standard equipment on the Deluxe model. The Morris 1100 Mark I models continued in production with relatively few changes until September 1967.

Standard equipment at launch for the Basic model included a driver's sun visor, front and rear parcel shelf, glove box, windscreen washers and front wheel disc brakes. Storage boxes on either side of the rear seats were fitted to two-door export models only. Deluxe models also had a temperature gauge,

passenger sun visor, front door bins for four-door models, over-riders, stainless steel window frames on doors, and a spare wheel!

Optional equipment included heater, seatbelts, leather trimmed seats, locking petrol cap, bonnet lock and an anti-mist rear window panel which was a popular accessory before heated rear windows became available. Estate models: Reclining front seats, leather trim, laminated windscreen, whitewall tyres, Weathermaster tyres.

PRODUCTION NUMBERS: from 1962 to 1969, 1100 saloons 510,000, 1100 estates 13,700, 1300 saloons 87,000, 1300 estates 10,800. From 1970 onwards accurate figures

Morris 1100 Mk I Traveller.

Manual gearchange layout.

Instrument layout.

are not available, but total production from 1962 to 1973 was approximately 700,000 saloons and 40,000 estates.

PRICES: 1965 Morris 1100 four-door saloon (Basic) £614, (Deluxe including heater) £644. Leather trim option £12.

COLOURS: Saloon, Old English White, Fiesta Yellow, Connaught Green, Tartan Red, Trafalgar Blue, Smoke Grey, Dove Grey, Black. Estate, Cumulus Grey, Trafalgar Blue, Maroon, Black.

ENGINE: Four-cylinder, OHV, bore 64.58mm, stroke 83.72mm, 1098cc (67.02in^3).

Maximum bhp 48 at 5100rpm. SU HS2 carburettor.

GEARBOX: Four-speed, floor-mounted gearchange, synchromesh on top three gears. Ratios: top 4.133, third 5.83, second 8.98, first 14.99, reverse 14.99. Front-wheel drive with helical spur gears and open drive shafts with universal joints, final drive ratio 4.133:1.

BRAKES: Lockheed with pressure limiting valve fitted to apportion more accurate braking between front and rear wheels. Front 8in discs, rear 8in drums.

STEERING: Rack and pinion.

TYRES: 5.50 x 12.

SUSPENSION: Front: Independent wishbone: Rear: Independent trailing arms and anti-roll bar, front and rear interconnected Hydrolastic displacers.

DIMENSIONS: Length: Deluxe 12ft 2.75in (3.73m); **width**: 5ft 0.4in (1.534m); **height**: 4ft 5in (1.35m); **wheelbase**: 7ft 9.5in (2.375m); **track**: front 4ft 3.375in (1.297m), rear 4ft 2.875in (1.272m); **ground clearance**: 6.5in (17cm); **turning circle**: 34ft (10.363m);

kerb weight: saloon, 16cwt 1qtr 9lb (830kg).

CAPACITIES: Fuel: 8 gallons (36.37 litres). Boot: saloon 9.5ft^3 (0.269m^3), estate 14ft^3 (0.4m^3) or 37.7ft^3 (1.07m^3) with rear seat folded down.

Morris 1100 Mk II, Morris 1300

The Morris 1100 range was expanded when the Mk II models were introduced in October 1967. Two-door models had previously been available for export markets, and there had been a two-door MG 1100 version. Two-door 1100 models were introduced to the home market. In addition, larger-engined 1275 cc two- and four-door 1300 models joined the range, along with a 1300 Traveller estate version. Specification differences and trim levels were now denoted as Deluxe and Super Deluxe.

The main external differences from the Mark I models were a wider front grille, higher front bumper, new rear light units mounted in

The 1971 model range.

chopped tail fins, side repeater indicator lamps on the front wings, twin number plate lights mounted on the rear bumper, and changes to the wheels which were now of the ventilated disc type. The grille pattern was different for 1100 and 1300 models, and the badging changed at the front and on the rear. Internal changes centred on the dash panel which, on the Deluxe model, had a central instrument

Sectioned Austin 1100 Estate.

Promotional image for the Mk II Morris 1300 Traveller.

Automatic Morris 1300 Mk II.

1098cc engine.

Morris 1300 GT

The sales success of the Morris 1100 and 1300 cars and the proliferation of models due to badge engineering prompted the introduction of a new model in October 1969 to broaden the appeal to those seeking a sportier car.

Austin and Morris four-door 1300 GT models were added to the range in October 1969. Mechanically they were similar to the Riley 1300 and MG 1300 Mk II models with the exception of the suspension, which was set slightly lower. However, they differed significantly from the rest of the range in terms of external appearance and internal trim. Apart from identifying badging and front grille differences the Austin and Morris GT models were identical. At launch three new exterior colours, Glacier White, Flame Red and Bronze Yellow were introduced, along with a matt black vinyl roof and black interior trim. Matt black featured extensively, being present on the mesh grille, along with two contrasting chrome strips and red GT script on the side mouldings, which had chrome outline finishers, and on the hub caps, which had chrome strakes. Internally a black vinyl-covered fascia comprising three dial instrumentation, black sun visors and a black rear view mirror added to the colour co-ordination. Reclining front seats were standard on GT models. The Morris 1300 GT model remained in production until 1971 when, as part of rationalisation within the Morris range, they were discontinued. Austin 1300 GT models continued with a new range of colours until 1974.

Standard equipment for the Deluxe

cluster flanked either side by an open parcel shelf. Super Deluxe models had a strip speedometer with rocker switchgear either side. On Morris models this had a matt black crackle finish. Corresponding Austin models had a matt silver finish. The Mk II Morris 1100 Traveller which, like its 1300 counterpart, sported a simulated wood grain full-length side finisher, only remained in production until 1968 when it was phased out. However, the 1300 version continued until 1971 when production of all Mk II Morris models ceased. Interestingly, although the colour range increased during the production run, on early models it was quite restricted, with only Snowberry White, Connaught Green and Tartan Red being available.

Morris 1300GT instrument layout.

included a heater, circular speedometer, full width front parcel shelf, two sun visors, windscreen washers, armrests on all doors, single lever on steering column for indicators, headlight flasher, dipswitch and horn (previously the dipswitch had been on the floor and the horn was a button in the middle of the steering wheel), plus front wing repeater indicators. The Super Deluxe had ribbon type speedometer with water temperature gauge, and, in addition to the Deluxe, pockets on all doors and rear quarter panels on two-door models, opening hinged rear window on two-door models, over-riders, The Traveller, in addition to the above, featured two wing mirrors, folding rear seat with removable base. GT models had in addition a revolution counter and reclining front seats.

Optional equipment included radio, seatbelts, auxiliary lights, reclining front seats, electrically heated rear window (saloon only),

Manual gearchange layout.

automatic transmission and over-riders, except Super Deluxe.

PRICES: 1969. 1100 Mk II two-door Deluxe saloon £739, 1300 two-door Super Deluxe saloon £792, 1100 Mk II four-door Deluxe saloon £792, 1300 four-door Super Deluxe saloon £818, 1300 Traveller £877, 1300 GT saloon £909.

COLOURS: Early cars: Snowberry White, Tartan Red, Connaught Green followed by Trafalgar Blue, Smoke Grey, Black. Later cars: Glacier White, Fawn Brown, Antelope, Bedouin, Limeflower, Flame Red, Connaught Green, Racing Green, Aqua, Bermuda Blue, Teal Blue, Blue Royale, Midnight Blue, Cumulus Grey. Some colours not available on all models.

ENGINE: Four-cylinder, OHV, 1100, bore 64.58mm, stroke 83.72mm, 1098cc (67.02in). Maximum bhp 48 at 5100rpm. SU HS2 carburettor. 1300, bore 70.61mm, stroke 81.28mm, 1275cc (77.82in^3), maximum bhp 58 at 5250rpm, SU HS4 carburettor. 1300 GT as 1300 except maximum bhp 70 at 6000rpm. Two SU HS2 carburettors.

GEARBOX: Four-speed, floor-mounted gearchange, synchromesh on top three gears (synchromesh on all gears from 1968), 1100 ratios top 4.133, third 5.83, second 8.97, first 15.0, reverse 15.0. Final drive ratio 4.133:1. 1300 ratios top 3.65, third 5.16, second 7.95, first 13.23, reverse 13.23. Final drive ratio 3.65:1. 1300 GT ratios top 3.65, third 5.23, second 8.09, first 12.89, reverse 12.89. Final drive ratio 3.65:1.

BRAKES: Lockheed with pressure limiting valve, front 8in discs, rear 8in drums. 1300 GT had 8in front discs with option of power assistance.

STEERING: Rack and pinion.

TYRES: 5.50 x 12, GT 145 x 12 radial ply tyres.

SUSPENSION: Front: Independent wishbone. Rear: Independent trailing arms and anti-roll bar, front and rear interconnected Hydrolastic displacers.

DIMENSIONS: **Length**: saloon and estate with over-riders, 12ft 2.75in (3.73m), GT and two-door without over-riders, 12ft 1.81in (3.69m); **ground clearance**: saloon 6.125in (15cm), estate 6.5in (17cm), GT and two-door, 5.75in (15cm); all other dimensions/weight as 1100 Mk I.

CAPACITIES: Fuel: 8 gallons (36.37 litres).

Boot: saloon 9.5ft^3 (0.269m^3), estate 14ft^3 (0.4m^3) or 37.7ft^3 (1.07m^3) with rear seat folded down.

Morris 1300 Traveller Mk III

The announcement of the Mk III models in September 1971 coincided with the discontinuation of the Morris Oxford Series VI models and the announcement that Morris Minor Travellers and vans would cease production at Adderley Park, Birmingham. The introduction of the new Morris Marina range in spring 1971 impacted greatly on the Morris 1100 and 1300 models. Although there was a full complement of Austin-badged two- and four-door saloons and estate versions, only the 1300 Traveller was retained as a Mk III Morris model. It was destined to remain in production for two years before being discontinued in April 1972 for UK sales, and in April 1973 for overseas markets. Riley 1300 models had been discontinued in 1969, while Wolseley 1300 models soldiered on until 1973. Vanden Plas and all Austin models were phased out in June 1974, thus bringing to an end a successful 12-year production run during which over two million vehicles of all marques and variants were produced.

The Mk III Morris Traveller had many new features, amongst which was a new front grille consisting of triple bright steel strips on a black mesh similar to that used for the 1300 GT that had been released as a Mark II model in 1969. It replaced the more elaborate designs seen on the earlier 1100/1300 models. Front and rear badges were also changed. Other external changes included a revised front bumper without over-riders, the removal of the indicator repeater flashers from the front wings, and the use of a single teardrop number plate light. Internal changes included a completely new simulated wood grain dashboard housing two circular instrument dials, revised switches, a glove box and swivelling fresh air vents positioned at each end. Improved wider seats with a pleated pattern, thicker carpets, and a smaller, padded, 15in steering wheel were new

Sole survivor! Only the Traveller models were designated Mk III.

Standard equipment included simulated wood grain dashboard with circular instruments comprising speedometer, fuel and water temperature gauges, combined key operated ignition/starter switch with steering column lock, heater, windscreen washers, opening quarter lights in front doors, glove box on passenger-side plus armrests on all doors. Factory fitted static or automatic seatbelts were available at extra cost, but had to be specified at the point of purchase.
Optional extras: Automatic transmission, reclining front seats, radial ply tyres.

additions to the specification. Mechanically there were further amendments including changing the electrical system to negative earth and replacing the dynamo with an alternator.

PRICES: 1971. £976, 1972. £1069.

COLOURS: Glacier White, Flame Red, Blaze, Midnight Blue, Teal Blue, Aqua, Black Tulip, Green Mallard, Harvest Gold, Limeflower, Bronze Yellow Damask Red.

ENGINE: This and the following are 1971 specifications. Four-cylinder, OHV, bore 70.61mm, stroke 81.28mm, 1275cc (77.82in³). Maximum bhp 60 at 5250rpm. SU HS4 carburettor.

GEARBOX: Four-speed all synchromesh, floor-mounted gearchange. Ratios: top 3.65, third 5.22, second 8.10, first 12.88, reverse 12.92. Front-wheel drive with helical spur gears and open drive shafts with universal joints, final drive ratio 3.65:1.

BRAKES: Lockheed, front 8in discs, rear 8in drums.

STEERING: Rack and pinion.

TYRES: 5.50 x 12, spare wheel in covered recess under boot floor.

SUSPENSION: Front: Independent wishbone. Rear: Trailing arms, front and rear interconnected Hydrolastic displacers.

DIMENSIONS: **Length**: 12ft 1.81in (3.69m); **width**: 5ft 6.875in (1.70m); **height**: 4ft 8in (1.42m); **wheelbase**: 93.5in; all other dimensions as 1100 Mark I; **weight**: 16cwt 3qtr 4lb (853kg).

CAPACITIES: Fuel: 8 gallons (36.37 litres). Boot: 14ft³ (0.4m³), with rear seat folded down 37.7ft³ (1.07m³).

Morris 1800 Mk I

BMC's Issigonis-designed 1800 model was introduced in 1964 as an Austin. Morris versions did not appear until March 1966. Destined to be known as the 'Landcrab,' this large saloon represented a departure from the contemporary rear-wheel drive Farina Morris Oxford Series VI models, which remained in production until 1971. The front-wheel drive 1800 Mk I models were noted for their spacious cabin space, Hydrolastic suspension, and all-synchromesh gearbox. The transversely mounted 1798cc B series engine had derived from the 1622cc version used in the Oxford, with the extra capacity produced by increasing the bore from 76.2mm to 80.26mm. Mechanically, the Austin and Morris Mk I versions were identical, the

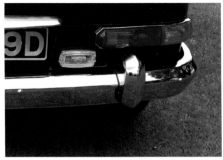

The Wipac reversing lights are an owner-added extra.

Simplistic rear badging and horizontal rear lights set the Mk I models apart.

1800 instrument layout.

1800 Mk I engine bay. Note the transverse location of the engine, with the radiator against the front wing instead of the grille.

major difference in appearance being limited to badging, grille design and rear lighting styles. A badge-engineered Wolseley 18/85 version was introduced in 1967. Distinctive differences included marque badging, a typical Wolseley front grille, and revised rear lights.

The specifications for Standard models included a full-width front parcel shelf, dashboard with padded top, driver's sun visor, headlamp flasher and side repeater indicators, and an interior boot lamp. Deluxe models featured a passenger sun visor, heater, arm rests on the door, rear seat centre arm rest, opening front quarter lights and over-riders. Optional extras included fresh air heater, reclining front seats, and a radio. Instrumentation included ribbon type speedometer with mileage trip, combined water temperature and fuel gauges, and warning lights to show low oil pressure and a dirty oil filter.

Mk I models continued in production until March 1968 when they were replaced by the Mk II version.

PRODUCTION NUMBERS: All Morris 1800/2200 models from 1966 to 1975,

approximately 95,271. Morris 1800 Mk I estimated number 24,000.

PRICES: 1966. Morris 1800 saloon £832, Deluxe £872. Optional extras: reclining front seats £18, fresh air heater £15.

COLOURS (1966): Introductory colours. Smoke Grey, Mandalay Grey, Danube Blue, Arianca Beige, Cumulus Grey.

COLOURS (1967): Connaught Green, Alaskan Blue, Maroon B, Arianca Beige, Old English White.

ENGINE: Four-cylinder, OHV, bore 80.26mm, stroke 88.9mm, 1798cc (109.8in^3). Maximum bhp 84 at 5000rpm. SU HS6 carburettor.

GEARBOX: Four-speed, floor-mounted gearchange operated by flexible cables, synchromesh on top three gears. Ratios: top 3.882, third 5.37, second 8.61, first 12.77, reverse 11.93. Front-wheel drive with helical spur gears and open drive shafts, final drive ratio 3.882:1.

BRAKES: Power assisted with pressure limiting valve, front 9.281in discs, rear 9in drums. Handbrake mounted under dashboard.

STEERING: Rack and pinion, early cars power assisted.

TYRES: 175mm x 13in. Note: mixed metric and imperial measurements was something that appeared with the introduction of radial ply tyres

SUSPENSION: Front: Independent with upper and lower arms with tie rods, swivel axles mounted on ball joints. Rear: Independent with trailing arms, front and rear interconnected with Hydrolastic displacers.

DIMENSIONS: **Length**: 13ft 8.18in (4.17m); **width**: 5ft 6.87in (1.7m); **height**: 4ft 8in 1.42m); **wheelbase**: 8ft 10in (2.69m); **track**: front 4ft 8in (1.43m), rear 4ft 7.5in (1.41m); **ground clearance**: 6.625in (17cm); **turning circle**: 37ft (11.3m); **weight**: 1ton 2cwt 2qtr 14lb (1150kg).

CAPACITIES: Fuel: 10.5 gallons (47.7 litres). Boot: 17ft^3 (0.48m^3)

Morris 1800 Mk II

Introduced in May 1968, the 1800 Mk II featured a revised front grille, a changed indicator/sidelight arrangement, and restyled rear lights with the housing fitted

Mk II models featured revised body styling to accommodate different lighting arrangements and a new front grille.

vertically instead of horizontally. The rear wings had a changed profile, and both Morris and Austin cars not only shared the same style of rear lights but were identical in all respects except for badging. The Wolseley 18/85 retained its own frontal arrangement and unique rear lights. Other changes for

the 1800 Mark II included slight tweaks to the engine with improved cylinder head breathing and a higher compression ratio, 14in wheels with narrower section tyres

77

Mk I.

Mk II.

Mk II S.

Mk III 1800.

Mk III 2200.

Gearchange layout is the same for all models.

than those fitted to the earlier 13in wheels on the Mk I. Internal changes centred on the addition of a simulated wood grain fascia, the inclusion of two-speed wipers and electrically operated screen washers, revisions to the interior door controls and door bins, a change to a combined steering column-mounted stalk for the dip switch, the headlight flasher and the horn. Power assisted steering was available as an optional extra, as was a radio, reclining front seats, a three-bar electrically heated rear window and automatic transmission.

Morris 1800 Mk II 'S'

In October 1968 an additional model was added to the range. Designated as the Mk II 'S', externally it looked identical to the Mk II except for the distinctive badging on the front grille and the boot lid. A further distinguishing feature, in the shape of a full length contrasting anodised aluminium side strip, was added later. Mechanically, however, it offered much more. A more powerful 96bhp version of the 1.8 B series engine sported twin SU HS6 carburettors, a three-branch manifold, tuned exhaust system and a high lift camshaft. Stopping power was enhanced by servo assisted larger front disc and pads, and with a maximum speed approaching 100mph they

'S' models are recognisable by the anodised aluminium side stripe.

were certainly needed. It is estimated that 46,000 Mk II models were built by the time production ended in 1972.

PRICES (1971): Morris 1800 Mk II Deluxe saloon £1193, Morris 1800 Mk II Deluxe saloon £1255, seatbelts (automatic front) £12, seatbelts (static front) £6.50. Optional extras: reclining front seats £18.75, heated rear screen £12.50, power assisted steering £43.75, automatic transmission £100.
COLOURS (1968): Cumulus Grey, Connaught Green, Porcelain Green, Persian Blue, Blue Royale, Damask Red, Faun Brown, Snowberry White.
COLOURS (1971): Green Mallard, Midnight Blue, Teal Blue, Damask Red, Harvest Gold, Limeflower, Wild Moss, Glacier White.
ENGINE: Four-cylinder, OHV, bore 80.26mm, stroke 88.9mm, 1798cc (109.8in^3), maximum bhp 86.5 at 5400rpm. SU HS6 carburettor. 'S' model maximum bhp 95.5 at 5700rpm. Two SU HS6 carburettors.
GEARBOX: Four-speed, floor-mounted gearchange operated by flexible cables, synchromesh on top three gears. Ratios top 3.882, third 5.35, second 7.98, first 12.77, reverse 11.93. Front-wheel drive with helical spur gears and open drive shafts, final drive ratio 3.882:1.
BRAKES: Power assisted with pressure limiting valve, front 9.281in discs, rear 9in drums. 'S' model front 9.7in discs, rear 9in drums. Handbrake mounted under dashboard.
STEERING: Rack and pinion, power assistance optional.
TYRES: 165 x 14, spare wheel in a wind down tray under boot floor.

SUSPENSION: Front: Independent with upper and lower arms with tie rods, swivel axles mounted on ball joints. Rear: Independent with trailing arms, front and rear interconnected with Hydrolastic displacers.
DIMENSIONS: **Length**: 13ft 10.875 (4.24m); **width**: 5ft 6.875in (1.7m); **height**: 4ft 8in (1.42m); **wheelbase**: 8ft 10in (2.69m); **track**: front 4ft 8in (1.43m), rear 4ft 7.5in (1.41m); **ground clearance**: 6.625in (17cm); **turning circle**: 37ft (11.3m); **weight**: 1ton 2cwt 2qtr 14lb (1150kg).
CAPACITIES: Fuel: 10.5 gallons (47.7 litres). Boot: 17ft^3 (0.48m^3).

Morris 1800 Mk III and 2200

The Austin-Morris Group within British Leyland heralded significant changes to the Austin-Morris 1800 range in March 1972. The Mk II 'S' models were dropped, and elsewhere within the company the Wolseley 18/85 variant was discontinued. The newly designated Mk III 1800 featured yet another redesign of the front grille, and was shared between Austin and Morris cars. Other changes included a floor-mounted handbrake between the front seats, improved instrumentation in closer proximity to the driver, and the introduction of a combined key start with a steering column lock. Mechanical changes were minimal, but an alternator was now fitted rather than a dynamo, and there was an improved gearchange courtesy of a rod- rather than a cable-operated system.

New Austin, Morris and Wolseley models were introduced simultaneously. Austin and Morris models became the 2200 models, and the Wolseley became the Six – a clear reference to the six-cylinder 2227cc engine fitted to all three variants. The 2200 replaced the 'S' models in both the Morris and Austin range. The six-cylinder engine was derived from the four-cylinder E series Austin Maxi 1500 engine and not as might have been expected from the six-cylinder C series engine that had been used in the Austin Westminster. Fitting the transverse overhead camshaft engine into the spacious engine bay and marrying it up to the revised gearbox

Morris 1800 Mk III.

arrangement was accomplished with ease. Engine performance was widely praised, with brisk acceleration times, 110bhp, and a maximum speed of 104mph. Niggles were few, but some questioned the fuel economy of the larger power unit, especially in power down mode. Externally, the 2200 can be identified by its different front grille, distinctive badging, and absence of the anodised aluminium side trim of the 'S' model it replaced. Standard equipment included water temperature gauge, simulated wood grain trimmed dashboard with padded top, twin pocket front parcel shelf, headlight flasher, combined steering column lock and ignition/starter switch, side repeater indicators, two sun visors, opening quarter

lights, and more. Additions to the 2200 specification included an oil pressure gauge, reclining front seats, and a larger capacity fuel tank. Over-riders that had previously been standard equipment were no longer fitted to any model. Optional extras included a radio, reclining front seats (1800 only), five-bar electrically heated rear window, power assisted steering, automatic transmission, metallic paint, and Rostyle wheels (2200 only). During 1974 an electrically heated rear window, driver's door mirror and hazard warning lights became standard equipment on both models. Production of all models ceased in March 1975, by which time it was estimated that 95,271 Morris 1800 and 2200 cars had been

Over-riders were dropped from the specification on 1800 Mk III and 2200 models.

Morris 2200 Mk III.

built since the launch of the Morris 1800 range in 1966.

PRODUCTION NUMBERS: Estimated that 23,000 Morris 1800 and 2200 Mk III models were built.

COST IN 1973: For the 1973 model year an optional 1973 extras pack was offered for both 1800 and 2200 models at extra cost. Morris 1800 Deluxe saloon £1287. Morris 1800 Deluxe saloon with 1973 extras pack £1299. Pack included exterior mirror, hazard warning lights, heated rear window and cigar lighter. Morris 2200 Deluxe saloon £1426. Morris 2200 Deluxe saloon with 1973 extras pack £1461. Pack included reclining front seats,

Manual gearchange layout.

Morris 2200 instrument layout.

exterior mirror, hazard warning lights, heated rear window and cigar lighter.

COLOURS (1972): Black Tulip, Glacier White, Limeflower, Damask Red, Midnight Blue, Green Mallard, Teal Blue, Harvest Gold, Lagoon Metallic and Rheingold Metallic.

COLOURS (1974): Mirage, Tundra, Aconite, Damask Red, Bracken, Harvest Gold, Glacier White and the following metallics: Cosmic Blue, Lagoon Blue, Brazil, Rheingold.

ENGINE: 1800, four-cylinder, OHV, bore 80.26mm, stroke 88.9mm, 1798cc (109.8in³). Maximum bhp 86.5 at 5400rpm. SU HS6 carburettor. 2200, six-cylinder, OHC, bore 76.2mm, stroke 81.28mm, 2227cc (135.8in³). Maximum bhp 110 at 5250rpm. Two SU HS6 carburettors (late models had two SU HIF6 carburettors).

GEARBOX: Four-speed all synchromesh, floor-mounted rod-operated gearchange. Ratios top 3.88, third 5.35, second 7.99, first 12.77, reverse 11.91. Front-wheel drive with helical spur gears and open drive shafts, final drive ratio 3.88:1, optional automatic 4.19:1.

BRAKES: Power assisted with pressure limiting valve, front 9.281in discs, rear 9in drums.

2200 front 9.7in discs, rear 7in drums. Floor-mounted handbrake.

STEERING: Rack and pinion, power assistance optional.

TYRES: 165 x 14.

SUSPENSION: Front: Independent with upper and lower arms with tie rods, swivel axles mounted on ball joints. Rear: Independent with trailing arms, front and rear interconnected with Hydrolastic displacers.

DIMENSIONS: Length: 13ft 10.21in (4.22m); **width**: 5ft 6.875in (1.7m); **height**: 4ft 8.17in (1.43m); **wheelbase**: 8ft 10in (2.69m); **track**: front 4ft 8in (1.43m), rear 4ft 7.5in (1.41m); **ground clearance**: 6.42in (16cm); **turning circle**: 37ft (11.3m); **approximate weights**: 1800, 1ton 2cwt 3qtr (1155kg), 2200, 1ton 3cwt 1qtr 13lb (1187kg).

CAPACITIES: Fuel: 1800 10.5 gallons (47.7 litres), 2200 12.5 gallons (56.8 litres). Boot: 17ft³ (0.48m³).

Morris 18-22 Series

The 18-22 range of vehicles announced in March 1975 included Austin, Morris and Wolseley models. The cars were an all-new

This is the first ADO71 model built. It was retained by British Leyland until 1977 when it was first registered. Restored to present condition in 2016.

design and differed in body profile from anything that had gone before in the Morris range. Designed by Harris Mann who was responsible for the Austin Allegro and the TR7, the 18-22 models stood apart, and became noteworthy for their streamlined,

Gearchange layout.

Instrument layout, HL models.

wedge-shaped look. However, the Morris and Wolseley versions were destined to be in production for a mere six months due to a rationalisation that resulted in them being axed along with the Austin version in September 1975. The models which followed were known as the Leyland Princess and these were destined to be replaced by the Ambassador models which were badged as Austin. A consequence of the short-lived production run for the Morris-badged 18-22 models is that they are exceptionally rare today.

The Morris models, like the rest of

Sunroof is an owner-added extra.

The number of surviving Morris 18/22 models is estimated to be in single figures

the range, comprised 1800, 1800HL and 2200HL versions. An innovative feature on all these models was the Hydragas suspension system designed by Alex Moulton, which had previously been used by Harris Mann in the Austin Allegro. This system, which superseded the Hydrolastic suspension used on earlier front-wheel drive Morris cars, utilised pressurised nitrogen units instead of rubber cones, and was interconnected front and rear. An element of continuity from previous 1800 and 2200 models was provided by the continued use of the 1798cc four-cylinder overhead valve engine on the 1800 models, and the 2227cc six-cylinder overhead cam engine on the 2200 cars. While the advertising department may have revelled in the slogan on the Morris Brochures 'The car that has got it all together' and emphasised styling,

performance, luxury and safety, in the case of the Morris Badged cars it was for an all too brief period. Externally the Morris and Wolseley models differed from their Austin counterparts because of the raised centre panel on the bonnet, the four-headlamp arrangement and marque badging.

Standard equipment included water temperature gauge, padded dashboard, heater/demister with three-speed fan, front and rear parcel shelves, lockable glove box, reclining front seats, height adjustable driver's seat, armrests on all doors, dipping rear view mirror, inertia reel front seatbelts, heated rear window, two-speed wipers with flick wipe and electric windscreen washers controlled by a single lever on the side of the steering column, interior bonnet release, two exterior mirrors, reversing lights, hazard warning lights. The HL model also had battery condition meter, clock, rear seat folding armrest, floor console surrounding the gearlever, passenger vanity mirror, lockable fuel filler cap, coachline, wheel trim rings, vinyl covered rear quarter panels and bright door and wheelarch mouldings, aluminium sill tread strips, Amblair vinyl trim, grab rails and coat hooks. 2200 models had power assisted steering.

Optional extras: Dunlop Denovo run flat tyres, power assisted steering on 1800 models, laminated windscreen, tinted glass, head rests, and automatic transmission. HL models only. Radio and full vinyl covered roof.

PRICE ON INTRODUCTION: Morris 1800 £2116, Morris 1800HL £2214, Morris 2200HL £2424.
COLOURS: Citron, Tahiti Blue, Damask Red, Flamenco, Harvest Gold, Glacier White and the following metallics: Cosmic Blue, Lagoon, Brazil, Reynard.
ENGINE: 1800, four-cylinder, OHV, bore 80.26mm, stroke 89mm, 1798cc (109.8in^3). Maximum bhp 82 at 5200rpm. SU HS6 carburettor. 2200, six-cylinder, OHC, bore 76.2mm, stroke 81.28mm, 2227cc (135.8in^3). Maximum bhp 110 at 5250rpm. Two SU HIF6 carburettors.
GEARBOX: Four-speed all synchromesh, floor-mounted gearchange. Ratios: top 3.72, third 5.13, second 7.66, first 12.24, reverse 11.42.

Front-wheel drive with helical spur gears and open drive shafts, final drive ratio 3.72:1, automatic 3.83:1.

BRAKES: Power assisted, front 10.6in discs, rear 9in drums. Floor-mounted handbrake.

STEERING: Rack and pinion, power assisted on 2200.

TYRES: 185/70 x 14.

SUSPENSION: Front: Independent, upper and lower transverse arms: Rear: Independent, trailing arms, front and rear with interconnected Hydragas displacers.

DIMENSIONS: **Length**: 14ft 7.41in (4.46m); **width**: 5ft 8.11in (1.73m); **height**: 4ft 7.48in (1.41m); **wheelbase**: 8ft 9.24in (2.67m); **track**: front 4ft 10in (1.47m), rear 4ft 9.36in (1.46m); **ground clearance**: 7.5in (19cm); **turning circle**: 37ft 6in (11.3m); **approximate weights**: 1800, 1ton 2cwt 3qtr 15lb (1160kg), 2200, 1ton 3cwt 2qtr 6lb (1197kg).

CAPACITIES: Fuel: 16 gallons (72.74 litres). Boot: 18.8ft^3 (0.532m^3).

Morris Oxford Series V

Introduced in March 1959 the Morris Oxford Series V was successor to the Morris Oxford Series III. Available as a four-door saloon in either standard or Deluxe specification at launch, the Pininfarina-designed body represented a significant change from the previous Oxford model. Straighter, flatter, more angular clean-cut lines accentuated by 'finned' rear wings, and larger internal and external dimensions set it apart and defined the new model range. Though seven inches longer than the Series III the wheelbase was increased by just two inches. Powered by the BMC B series 1498cc engine in combination with a four-speed gearbox, with the option of floor-mounted or column-mounted gearchange for the UK market, a maximum speed of 79mph and cruising speed of 50-60mph were easily managed. Allied to independent front suspension that operated with coil springs and wishbones, and rear suspension with semi-elliptic leaf springs, the brisk performance was matched by a comfortable ride. The comparable Austin model was the Austin A55

Cambridge, though MG, Riley and Wolseley variants of the Farina-styled cars were also produced.

The Morris model range was increased in September 1960 with the announcement of the 'Morris Oxford Traveller' Series V estate car, which had an all-steel body derived from the saloon model. A split rear tailgate with upper and lower hinged sections provided easy access to the spacious rear loading area, and provided excellent rearward vision, courtesy of an expansive rear window. The rear seat arrangement offered flexibility in terms of use, according to contemporary publicity. The rear seat base folded forward and the split rear squabs could be folded to provide a continuous loading area or to serve as a headrest for a double bed-sized sleeping compartment. Once again there was an Austin equivalent: the Austin Cambridge A55 Countryman.

Standard equipment included water temperature and oil pressure gauges, driver's sun visor, glove box with lid, pile carpets, bench-type front seat, folding centre armrest in front and rear seats, and armrests in the rear doors. Deluxe specification added a clock,

Farina styling evident on the Morris Oxford Series V.

heater, windscreen washers, passenger sun visor and over-riders. Optional extras included a radio and wheel rim embellishers and, on the Deluxe models only, duo-tone paint.

PRODUCTION NUMBERS: 87,432.
COST ON INTRODUCTION: March 1959: Standard saloon £863, Deluxe saloon £893; September 1960: Standard saloon £815, Deluxe Saloon £844, Traveller £929. Optional extras: Duo-tone paint £17, heater £17, radio £34.

Handbrake by the driver's seat was a common feature of 1960s cars.

Instrument layout.

Gearchange layout.

Morris Oxford rear light layout (l to r): Series V; Series VI Traveller; Series VI.

COLOURS: 1959. Black, Dark Grey, Blue Grey, Light Green, Off White, Blue. Deluxe models: (single tone) Black, Dark Green, Maroon, Blue; (duo-tone, top colour listed first) Black/Dark Grey, Dark Grey/Blue Grey, Dark Green/Light Green, Maroon/Off White, Blue/Off White.

COLOURS: 1960/61. Black, Smoke Grey, Pearl Grey, Yukon Grey, Damask Red, Porcelain Green, Clipper Blue. Duo-tone (1961) Yukon Grey/Old English White, Porcelain Green/Connaught Green, Clipper Blue/Old English White, Pearl Grey/Maroon. Traveller models 1961: (single tone) Smoke Grey, Porcelain Green, Pearl Grey, Yukon Grey; (duo-tone) Smoke Grey/Clipper Blue, Pearl Grey /Maroon, Porcelain Green/Connaught Green.

ENGINE: Four-cylinder, OHV, bore 73.025mm, stroke 88.9mm, 1489cc (90.88in^3). Maximum bhp 53 at 4350rpm. SU carburettor.

GEARBOX: Four-speed, floor- or steering

column-mounted gearchange, synchromesh on top three gears. Ratios: saloon, top 4.55,

Morris Oxford Series V saloon with duo-tone exterior colour.

third 6.25, second 10.08, first 16.55, reverse 21.64; estate top 4.875, third 7.26, second 11.75, first 19.23, reverse 25.15.
REAR AXLE: Hypoid, three-quarter floating, ratio saloon 4.55:1, estate 4.875:1.
BRAKES: Girling, front and rear 9in drums.
STEERING: Cam and peg.
TYRES: 5.90 x 14.
SUSPENSION: Front: Independent with coil springs and wishbones. Rear: Semi-elliptic leaf springs with rubber mountings, piston type shock absorbers all round.
DIMENSIONS: Length: 14ft 10.125in (4.52m); **width**: 5ft 3.5in (1.61m); **height**: 4ft 11.75in (1.52m); **wheelbase**: 8ft 3.1875in (2.52m); **track**: front 4ft 0.56in (1.23m), rear 4ft 1.875in (1.267m); **ground clearance**: 6.25in (16cm); **turning circle**: 37ft 6in (11.43m); **weight**: 1ton 1cwt 2qtr (1092kg); estate as above except, **length**: 14ft 9.75in (4.51m); **weight**: 1ton 2cwt 2qtr (1143kg).
CAPACITIES: Fuel: 10 gallons (45.4 litres). Boot: saloon 19ft^3 (0.538 litres), estate with rear seat folded down 51.1ft^3 (1.446m^3).

Morris Oxford Series VI

The Morris Oxford Series VI saloon and Traveller estate models were introduced as replacements for the Series V models in October 1961. External body styling changes were confined to the front grille, bumpers and over-riders, the rear wings and rear lamp clusters. Frontal lighting changes included sealed beam headlamps and restyled and repositioned sidelight and indicator lamps.

Mechanically the major change from the previous model was the introduction of a larger 1662cc B series engine with an increased power output of 61bhp at 4500rpm. Three gearchange options were available: a floor-mounted four-speed, a column-mounted four-speed, and a Borg-Warner model 35 automatic option with a column-mounted selector.

A number of modifications designed to improve the ride and stability of the Series VI were introduced, including widening the track and lengthening the wheelbase, adding an anti-roll bar to the front and a stabilising bar to the

Series VI saloon, with owner-added, non-standard louvered bonnet.

rear, as well as stronger Armstrong heavy-duty shock absorbers and stronger rear springs.

Specifications for the Traveller estate car were identical to the saloon apart from changed final drive ratios from 4.875:1 to 4.55:1 and then 4.3:1 which were aimed at compensating for the heavier body and increased payload. Further continuity was maintained by leaving the rear body styling unchanged from the previous Series V model.

Series VI front view, with standard bonnet and badging.

Instrument layout.

 Gearchange layout.

In 1962 a diesel version of the 1498cc engine became available for the Series VI. It proved to be a popular choice for taxi drivers.

The Morris Oxford Series VI remained in production until 1971 with the Traveller estate being phased out in February and the saloon in April, along with the Wolseley 16/60. Previously, the MG Magnette had been discontinued in 1968 and the Austin Cambridge and Riley 4/72 in 1969.

Standard equipment included water temperature and oil pressure gauges, a lockable glove box, parcel tray, folding armrests in front and rear seats and

Series VI saloon with Austin Countryman estate.

armrests on rear doors, deluxe specification added a clock, a heater and windscreen washers. The Traveller estate in addition to standard saloon had two wing-mounted mirrors.

Optional extras included a radio, seatbelts,

column gearchange, Borg-Warner automatic transmission and rim embellishers. Deluxe models had the option of duo-tone paint colours. In 1964 the list of optional extra included duo-tone body colours, automatic transmission, Weathermaster tyres, whitewall tyres and a laminated windscreen. For Deluxe and Standard specification saloon and estate models a heater.

PRODUCTION NUMBERS: 208,823.
PRICES ON INTRODUCTION: October 1961: Standard saloon £868, Deluxe saloon £898, Traveller £992. May 1962: Standard saloon £819, Deluxe saloon £846, Traveller £936. Optional extras (May 1962): Automatic transmission £93, heater (fresh air type) £17, duo-tone paint saloon £11, Traveller £17.
COLOURS (1962 TRAVELLER): Dove Grey, Smoke Grey, Highway Yellow, Almond Green. Duo-tone colours, upper body colour first, Dove Grey/Rose Taupe, Smoke Grey/Old English White, Highway Yellow/Old English White, Almond Green/Dove Grey and all single tone body colours were available with Black roof.
COLOURS (1964 TRAVELLER): Dove Grey, Smoke Grey, Almond Green, Trafalgar Blue, Maroon, Black.
Duo-tone colours, upper body colour first, as 1962 except Trafalgar Blue/Old English White replaced Highway Yellow/Old English White.
COLOURS (1967 SALOON): Dove Grey, Trafalgar Blue, Maroon, Old English White. Duo-tones, all with Old English White roof and rear pillars, Smoke Grey, Rose Taupe, Almond Green.
COLOURS (1967 TRAVELLER): Dove Grey, Trafalgar Blue, Maroon. Duo-tone colours, upper body colour first, Smoke Grey/Old English White, Almond Green/Dove Grey.
COLOURS (1969 SALOON): Cumulus Grey, Blue Royale, Connaught Green, Damask Red, El Paso Beige, Fawn Brown, Glacier White.
ENGINE: Four-cylinder, OHV, bore 76.2mm, stroke 88.9mm, 1622cc (98.94in^3), maximum bhp 61 at 4500rpm. SU carburettor.
GEARBOX: Four-speed, floor- or steering column-mounted gearchange, synchromesh on top three gears. Ratios: saloon, top 4.3, third 5.91, second 9.52, first 15.64, reverse 20.45; estate top 4.3, third 6.25, second 10.08, first 16.55, reverse 21.64.

REAR AXLE: Hypoid, three-quarter floating, ratio saloon and estate 4.3:1
ENGINE (DIESEL): Four-cylinder, OHV, bore 73mm, stroke 89mm, 1489cc. Maximum 40bhp at 4000rpm. CAV fuel-injection.
GEARBOX: Four-speed, floor-mounted gearchange, synchromesh on top three gears. Ratios: top 4.55, third 6.78, second 10.93, first 17.95, reverse 23.47.
REAR AXLE: Hypoid bevel, ratio 4.55:1
BRAKES: Girling, front and rear 9in drums.
STEERING: Cam and peg.
TYRES: Saloon and Traveller 5.90 x 14.
SUSPENSION: Front: Independent with coil springs and wishbones, anti-roll bar. Rear: Semi-elliptic leaf springs with rubber mountings, stabiliser bar (saloon only), piston type shock absorbers all round.
DIMENSIONS: **Length**: 14ft 6.5in (4.43m); **width**: 5ft 3.5in (1.61m); **height**: 4ft 10.875in (1.49m); **wheelbase**: 8ft 4.25in (2.54m); **track**: front 4ft 2.625in (1.28m), rear 4ft 3.375in (1.30m); **ground clearance**: 6.5in (16.5cm); **turning circle**: 37ft (11.27m); **weight**: 1ton 1cwt 2qtr (1092kg). Traveller as above except, **length**: 14ft 9.375in (4.52m); **height**: 5ft (1.52m); **weight**: 1ton 3cwt 1qtr (1181kg).
CAPACITIES: Fuel: 10 gallons (45.4 litres). Boot: saloon 19ft^3 (0.538m^3), Traveller with rear seat folded down 51.1ft^3, note there are two positions for Traveller folding rear seat, load carrying space 5ft 1.75in (1.57m) long or 5ft 11in (1.8m) long for sleeping accommodation.

Morris Marina Mark I

The Morris Marina entered production in April 1971. Work on the body design was initiated by Roy Haynes, who had previously worked for Ford, however, on his departure from British Leyland in 1970, the design work was completed by Harris Mann. On the occasion of the Diamond Jubilee of Morris in 1973, two years into Marina production by which time 300,000 had been produced, the publicity department lauded its virtues in a press release as follows: "When it appeared in 1971, the Marina was billed as 'beauty with brains behind it', a fair description.

This 1972 Morris Marina was recently donated to the British Motor Museum.

Marina launch models: four-door saloon and two-door coupé.

It combined the well-tried suspension characteristics and steering mechanism of the Minor 1000 with the celebrated and long-lived British Leyland B series engine and a svelte bodyshell styled at the Longbridge plant. Straightforward and brisk, inexpensive to buy and maintain and offered in attractive estate car and coupé and saloon versions, the Marina is essentially the kind of sensible, practical car that the name of Morris has conjured up for the past 60 years."

The Marina carried on the conventional rear-wheel drive tradition that had been adopted in the Morris Minor and Morris Oxford Series VI models that it replaced. It also bucked the badge engineering trend prevalent in BMC and British Leyland. Apart from American, Canadian and South African Austin-badged models, the Marina was marketed solely as a Morris throughout its production run in the UK.

When introduced the range consisted of four-door saloons and two-door coupés, with 1.3 Deluxe, 1.3 Super Deluxe, 1.8 Deluxe, 1.8 Super Deluxe and 1.8 TC options. In 1972 a 1.8 Super Deluxe four-door estate joined the model line-up.

Interestingly, the coupé used the same front doors as the saloon. Normally, a two-door car would have wider front doors than a four-door to make access to the rear of the car easier, but this convention was dispensed with in the case of the Marina.

Standard equipment included water temperature gauge, heater/demister with single-speed fan, front and rear full width parcel shelves, a rubber floor covering, interior bonnet release, two-speed wipers with flick wipe and electric windscreen washers controlled by a lever on the left side of the steering column. A lever on the right side controlled the horn, headlight flasher, dip switch and indicators, and there was a

Morris Marina TC Jubilee model marked 60 years of Morris.

TC instrument layout.

Gearchange layout.

combined ignition/starter switch incorporating steering lock. Super Deluxe models had in addition pile carpets instead of a rubber floor covering, tachometer, wheel trims and stainless wheelarch trims. TC models had in addition to Super Deluxe, folding centre armrest in rear seat, reversing lights and power assisted brakes and an alternator. In 1972 reclining seats and a heated rear screen were added. Optional extras (all other models) reclining front seats, heated rear window, alternator, automatic transmission; (1.3 and 1.8 only) reversing lights, larger tyres; (1.8 only) power assisted brakes. In 1974 an exterior mirror, hazard warning lights and heated rear window became standard equipment on all models.

PRODUCTION NUMBERS: All Marina/Ital models 1,338,392.
PRICES (1972): Morris Marina 1.3 two-door coupé Deluxe £958 Super Deluxe £998; Morris Marina 1.3 four-door saloon Deluxe £998 Super Deluxe £1038; Morris Marina 1.8 two-door coupé Deluxe £1023 Super Deluxe £1075; Morris Marina 1.8 four-door saloon Deluxe £1063 Super Deluxe £1115; Morris

Austin Marina 1.8 North American specification.

Marina 1.8 TC two-door coupé £1234; Morris Marina 1.8 TC four-door saloon £1273; Morris Marina 1.8 Super Deluxe Estate £1236.

COLOURS (1971): Glacier White, Blaze, Flame Red, Midnight Blue, Teal Blue, Aqua, Black Tulip, Green Mallard, Harvest Gold, Limeflower, Wild Moss, Bronze Yellow.

COLOURS (1974): Glacier White, Blaze, Bracken, Damask Red, Aconite, Teal Blue (not TC), Mirage, Tundra, Harvest Gold, Citron. TC in addition to above, Cosmic, Lagoon, Brazil, Rheingold (all metallics).

ENGINE: All four-cylinder, OHV. 1.3, bore 70.61mm, stroke 81.28mm, 1275cc (77.8in^3). Maximum bhp 60 at 5250rpm. SU HS4 carburettor. 1.8, bore 80.2mm, stroke 88.9mm, 1798cc (109.7in^3), maximum bhp 82.5 at 5250rpm. SU HS6 carburettor. TC as 1.8 except maximum bhp 94.5 at 5500rpm. Two SU HS4 carburettors.

GEARBOX (1971): Four-speed all synchromesh, floor-mounted gearchange. Ratios: 1.3, top 4.11, third 5.89, second 8.68, first 14.03, reverse 15.43. 1.8 and TC, top 3.64, third 4.75, second 7.00, first 11.31, reverse 12.44.

GEARBOX (1973): Four-speed all synchromesh, floor-mounted gearchange. Ratios 1.3, top 4.11, third 5.877, second 8.672, first 14.015, reverse 15.413. 1.8 and

Promotional material for Austin Marina models.

TC, top 3.64, third 4.768, second 7.025, first 11.32, reverse 12.45.
REAR AXLE: Hypoid bevel, ratios 1.3, 4.11:1, 1.8 and TC, 3.64:1.
BRAKES: 1.3, 8in front and rear drums, 1.8 and TC, front 9.79in discs, rear 8in drums, TC only power assisted.
STEERING: Rack and pinion.
TYRES: 1.3 5.20 x 13, 1.8 145 x 13, TC 165/70 x 13, optional 1.3 145 x 13, 1.8 165/70 x 13.
SUSPENSION: Front independent, torsion bar, lever-type shock absorbers, rear semi-elliptic leaf springs, telescopic shock absorbers.
DIMENSIONS/WEIGHT: Saloon **length**: 13ft 10.12in (4.219m); **width**: Deluxe 5ft 4.56in (1.64m), Super and TC 5ft 4.81in (1.646m); **height**: 4ft 8.12in (1.425m), TC 4ft 7.88in (1.419m); **wheelbase**: 8ft (2.438m); **track**: front 1.3 4ft 4.38in (1.33m), 1.8 and TC 4ft 4in (1.321m), rear 4ft 4in (1.321m); **ground clearance**: 1.3 5.75in (14.6cm), 1.8 5.52in (14.0cm), TC 5.42in (13.8cm); **turning circle**: 31ft (9.45m); **weight**: 1.3 17cwt 1qtr 4lb (878kg), 1.8 19cwt (964kg), TC 19cwt 8lb (968kg). Coupé as saloon except **length**: 13ft 7.12in (4.143m); **width**: Deluxe 5ft 4.36in (1.635m), Super and TC 5ft 4.61in

(1.641m); **height**: 4ft 7.35in (1.406m), TC 4ft 7.1in (1.40m); **weight**: 1.3 16cwt 2qtr 22lb (848kg), 1.8 18cwt 1qtr 16lb (934kg), TC 18cwt 2qtr (938kg). Note Super and TC featured wheelarch trim hence were marginally wider than the Deluxe model.
CAPACITIES: Fuel: 11.5 gallons (52.3 litres). Boot: saloon 13ft3 (0.378m^3), coupé 11ft^3 (0.32m^3), estate with rear seat folded down 58.4ft^3 (1.7m^3).

Morris Marina 2

By the time Morris introduced a series of upgrades to the Marina range in October 1975 with the announcement of the Morris Marina 2 models, the Marina was the only remaining Morris model in the British Leyland portfolio. The Mini had lost its Morris designation in 1969 and the Morris 1800 and 2200 models in the 18-22 Series had been rebranded as Leyland Princess in September 1975.

Revisions to the Marina models centred on improving the interior trim, instrumentation and levels of comfort. A curved dashboard arrangement was introduced, and this became a permanent feature until the end of

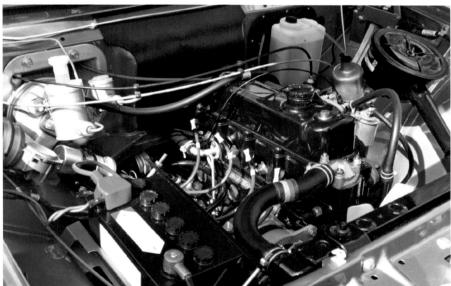

Morris Marina 2 1.8 Special four-door saloon (top) and 1.8 'B-Series' engine.

Morris Marina production and extended into its replacement, the Ital. Mechanically the engines remained the same as the Mark I, but improvements were made to the suspension resulting in improved handling and a more comfortable ride. Externally there were revised front grille arrangements for all models in the range. Model identity differed from the Mark I

(Top) Morris Marina 1.3 Deluxe Estate. (Bottom) Special Liveried LE (limited edition) model.

range and now included 1.3 Deluxe two- and four-door saloons, 1.3 Super two- and four-door saloons, 1.8 Super two- and four-door saloons and estate, 1.8 two- and four-door Special saloon, 1.8 two-door GT, and 1.8 HL four-door saloon. A 1.3 four-door Special saloon was added in 1977. Rear boot badges helped distinguish the different models.

Standard equipment included alternator, water temperature gauge, heater/demister with two-speed fan, glove box, front and rear parcel shelves, two sun visors with vanity mirror on passenger-side, pile carpets, armrests on all doors and rear quarter panel on two-door model, inertia reel front seatbelts, interior bonnet release, two-speed wipers with flick wipe and electric windscreen washers, single horn, headlight flasher, combined ignition/starter switch incorporating steering lock, heated rear window, reversing lights, hazard warning flashers, exterior door mirror. Super models had new seat trim, reclining front seats, wheel trims, stainless

side trim and cigarette lighter. Estate models had rear wash wipe and mud flaps for the rear wheels.

Special models had, in addition to Super, nylon fabric seat facings, head restraints, trip mileage recorder, clock, glove box light, simulated wood trim fascia inserts, twin horns, rear seat folding armrest, opening front quarter lights, boot light, two rectangular halogen driving lights, bright wheelarch mouldings, bumpers and under-riders with rubber inserts, and a vinyl roof. The highest specification models were the GT and HL models. Both had specially tuned engines capable of 85bhp and several distinguishing features. Both had, in addition to the Special models, a floor-mounted console, two door-mounted mirrors, additional instrumentation with increased numbers of warning lights, and extra lighting, including an engine compartment lamp. The GT had distinctive black side stripes, and wipers, window frames and rear panels all finished in matt black, as well as opening rear

Marina 2 Special (above) and GT (right) instrument layouts.

Gearchange layout.

windows, a heated rear screen and a chrome plated exhaust tail pipe. HL models sported halogen headlamps, tinted windows and a different more subtle coachline.

There was also an LE special edition with its own unique graphics and a vinyl roof. In 1976 a 1.3 Deluxe version of the estate was introduced. This was the first expansion to the estate range since its introduction in 1972. The Morris Marina 2 models remained in production until 1978

PRICES: 1975 Morris Marina 1.3 two-door Deluxe £1645, 1.3 two-door Super Deluxe £1724, 1.3 four-door Deluxe £1715, 1.3 four-door Super Deluxe £1794, 1.8 two-door Super Deluxe £186.1.8 four-door Super Deluxe £1931, 1.8 two-door Special £2008, 1.8 four-door Special £2068, 1.8 two-door GT £2146, 1.8 four-door HL £2217, 1.8 estate £2149.

COLOURS (1976): Deluxe and Super, Glacier White, Brooklands Green, Tahiti Blue, Damask Red, Flamenco, Sand Glow. Special, HL and GT, Glacier White, Damask Red, Flamenco, Sand Glow and the following metallics, Jade Green, Astral Blue, Brazil, Reynard.

ENGINE: All four-cylinder, OHV, 1.3, bore 70.61mm, stroke 81.28mm, 1275cc (77.8in^3). Maximum bhp 57 at 5550rpm. SU HS4 carburettor. 1.8, bore 80.2mm, stroke

88.9mm, 1798cc (109.7in³), maximum bhp 72 at 4750rpm. SU HS6 carburettor. HL and GT as 1.8 except maximum bhp 85 at 5500rpm and two SU HS4 carburettors.
GEARBOX: Four-speed all synchromesh, floor-mounted gearchange. Ratios 1.3, top 4.11, third 5.877, second 8.672, first 12.741, reverse 15.413. 1.8 all models, top 3.64, third 4.768, second 7.025, first 11.32, reverse 12.449.
REAR AXLE: Hypoid bevel, ratios 1.3, 4.11:1, 1.8, 3.64:1.
BRAKES: Front 9.79in discs, rear 8in drums, HL and GT only power assisted.
STEERING: Rack and pinion.
TYRES: 1.3 model 145 x 13, 1.8 all models 155 x 13.
SUSPENSION: Front independent, torsion bar, lever-type shock absorbers, rear semi-elliptic leaf springs, telescopic shock absorbers, front and rear anti-roll bar (not estate).
DIMENSIONS/WEIGHT: **Saloons length**: Deluxe and Super 14ft 0.68in (4.289m), Special and HL 14ft 1.8in (4.313m); **width**: Deluxe and Super 5ft 4.53in (1.639m), Special and HL 5ft 5.16in (1.655m); **height**: 1.3 saloon 4ft 7.91in (1.42m), 1.8 saloon 4ft 8.1in (1.425m); **two-door length**: Deluxe and Super 13ft 9.87in (4.213m), Special and GT 13ft 10.81in (4.237m); **width**: Deluxe and Super 5ft 4.41in (1.636m), Special and GT 5ft 5.04in (1.652m); **height**: 1.3 two-door 4ft 7.32in (1.405m), 1.8 two-door 4ft 7.51in (1.41m); **estate length**: 14ft 1.96in (4.317m); **width** 5ft 4.53in (1.639m); **height**: 4ft 8.61in (1.438m); **all models wheelbase**: 7ft 11.98in (2.438m); **track**: front and rear 4ft 4in (1.321m); **turning circle**: 31ft (9.45m); **saloons weight**: 1.3 17cwt 2qtr 10lb

(894kg), 1.8 Super 18cwt 2qtr 21lb (950kg), 1.8 Special 18cwt 3qtr 18lb (962kg), 1.8 HL 18cwt 3qtr 14lb (974kg), two-door 1.3 17cwt 1qtr 10lb (882kg), 1.8 Super 18cwt 1qtr 21lb (938kg), 1.8 Special 18cwt 2qtr 18lb (949kg) 1.8 GT 18cwt 3qtr 16lb (961kg). Estate 19cwt 2qtr 19lb (1000kg).
CAPACITIES: Fuel: 11.5 gallons (52.3 litres). Boot: four-door saloon 13ft³ (0.378m³), two-door saloon 11ft³ (0.32m³), estate 31.4ft³ (0.91m³) or 58.4ft³ (1.7m³) with rear seat folded down.

The VP Marina

Harris Mann was a talented, influential designer who contributed significantly to the styling of British Leyland cars including the prototype Marinas, the Allegro, TR7 and the 18-22 Series of vehicles later badged as the Leyland Princess range. At the time

What might have been? Harris Mann with his concept drawing for the VP Marina.

seriously considered as the starting point for a replacement Marina. Alternative design plans for the Marina Mk III were progressed and the VP Marina concept was shelved in favour of these. The VP concept drawings returned to Mann's archive but in recent times they have been shared, along with his personal recollections of their origins, with the marque's owners and enthusiasts.

Morris Marina Mark III

The Morris Marina Mark III model range, which had 11 models, was introduced in September 1978. The designation of the individual models was revised to include 1300 four-door saloon, two-door coupé and an estate, 1300 L four-door saloon and two-door coupé and a 1300 HL saloon. A new 1700 engine was introduced to replace the 1.8 used in the Marina 2 models. Five models were fitted with this engine: 1700 saloon and estate, 1700L saloon and estate and 1700 HL saloon. There were no 1700 two-door coupé models. The new overhead camshaft engine which had a five-bearing crank, belt-driven camshaft, side porting, a new piston design, and a twin downpipe exhaust system was promoted as being

that the Marina 2 was being phased out Harris Mann was completing work on a more radical and futuristic concept design for the Morris Marina. Dubbed the VP (Vanden Plas) Marina or, in his own words, the 'Posh' Marina, the designs came too late to be

Morris Marina Mk III 1300.

Instrument layout for Base and L models.

lighter, quieter and more compact than its predecessor, as well as being more economical.

Other changes from the Marina 2 models included a revised frontal arrangement with all models having two driving lamps incorporated into the front grille, and revised bumpers which incorporated the front indicators. At the rear

Morris Marina Mk III Base model estate.

Morris Marina Mk III 1700 HL.

the light clusters no longer wrapped around the rear wings. Another notable change was the removal of the front quarter lights. Three different levels of internal trim were assigned to basic, L and HL models and improvements were made to the fascia and general levels of instrumentation.

Standard equipment was generally as it had been for the Marina 2 models, and included alternator, water temperature gauge, trip mileage recorder, heater/demister with two-speed fan, face level ventilation, heated rear window, two driving lights, hazard warning lights, reversing lights, driver's door mirror. Estate models had a rear wiper/washer and a

1700 HL instrument layout.

tailgate lamp. L models added a clock, cigarette lighter, glove box light, reclining front seats, boot light. HL in addition to L model, halogen headlights, tinted glass, vinyl covered roof, triple coachline, all models now had rear fog lights, HL models had velour trimmed seats, intermittent windscreen wipe, front door bins

107

1700 L estate Mk III.

and 1700 HL had a push button radio. Optional extras included automatic transmission (L and HL saloon and estate models only), metallic paint finish, laminated windscreen, tinted glass where not fitted as standard, and vinyl roof appeared on 1300L and 1700 four-door models only. The Morris Marina Mark III models continued in production until 1980 when they were replaced by the Morris Ital.

PRICES FOR 1979 MODEL RANGE: Morris Marina 1300 two-door £2707, four-door £2822. 1300L two-door £2927, four-door £3006, 1300 HL four-door £3328, 1700 four-door £3029, 1700L four-door £3229, 1700 HL four-door £3555, 1300 estate £3218, 1700 estate £3378, 1700L estate £3615. 1700 HL estate was added to the range in April 1979 but was only available for 11 months. This addition increased the estate options to four, double the number in the Marina 2 range.

COLOURS (1979): Ermine White, Vermilion Red, Pageant Blue, Applejack, Russet Brown, Champagne, Sand Blow, Snapdragon. The following metallics (L and HL only), Silver, Tara Green, Oyster.

ENGINE: All four-cylinder, 1300 OHV, bore 70.61mm, stroke 81.28mm, 1275cc (77.8in^3). Maximum bhp 57 at 5500rpm. SU HS4 carburettor. 1700 OHC, bore 84.5mm, stroke 75.87mm, 1700cc (103.7in^3). Maximum bhp 78 at 5150rpm. SU HIF6 carburettor.

GEARBOX: Four-speed all synchromesh, floor-mounted gearchange. Ratios: 1300, top 4.11, third 5.877, second 8.672, first 14.015, reverse 15.413, 1700, top 3.64, third 4.768, second 7.025, first 11.32, reverse 12.45.

REAR AXLE: Hypoid bevel, ratio 1300 4.11:1, 1700 3.64:1.

BRAKES: All models, dual line, power assisted, 9.79in front discs, rear 8in drums.

STEERING: Rack and pinion. Two-spoke steering wheel (four-spoke on L and HL).

TYRES: 1300 saloon and coupé, 1300 L saloon 145 x 13, all other models 155 x 13.

SUSPENSION: Front independent, torsion bar, lever-type shock absorbers, rear semi-elliptic leaf springs, telescopic shock absorbers, front and rear anti-roll bars (not estate).

DIMENSIONS/WEIGHT: Saloon: **length**: 14ft 0.46in (4.28m), L and HL 14ft 0.93in (4.29m); **width**: 5ft 4.41in (1.64m); **height**: 4ft 7.91in (1.42m). Coupé: **length**: 13ft 9.45in (4.2m), L 13ft 9.92in (4.21m); **width**: 5ft 4.41in (1.64m), L 5ft 4.53in (1.64m); **height**: 4ft 7.32in (1.41m). Estate: **length**: 14ft 1.63in (4.31m), L 14ft 2.11in (4.32m); **width**: 5ft 4.53in (1.64m); **height**: 4ft 8.61in (1.44m). All models: **wheelbase**: 8ft (2.438m); **track**: front and rear 4ft 4in (1.321m); **turning circle**: 31ft (9.45m). Saloon: **weight**: 1300 17cwt 2qtr 13lb (895kg), 1300L 17cwt 2qtr 25lb (900kg), 1300HL 18cwt 10lb (919kg), 1700 18cwt 1qtr (927kg), 1700L 18cwt 1qtr 11lb (932kg), 1700HL 18cwt 3qtr 12lb (958kg). Coupé: **weight**: 17cwt 1qtr 15lb (883kg). Estate weight: 1300 19cwt 15lb (968kg), 1700 19cwt 2qtr 10lb (995kg), 1700L 19cwt 3qtr (1003kg), 1700HL 1ton 24lb (1027kg).
CAPACITIES: Fuel: 11.5 gallons (52.3 litres).

Morris Ital

The new model created to replace the Morris Marina was the Morris Ital. At its high-profile launch in June 1980 much was made of British Leyland's association with Giorgetto Guigiaro's Turin-based Italian design house,

Ital Design, in styling the car. However, the significant role of its own in-house designer Harris Mann was underplayed. Billed as 'Styled in Italy, built in Britain' at Michael Edwardes' insistence, the contemporary publicity failed to tell the full story. Though the Italian stylists did have an influence in making the Ital production line ready, at considerable cost, it was Harris Mann and his team of stylists who completed the final styling plans. Harris Mann, who had produced designs for an up-market version of the Marina when the Marina 2 was nearing the end of production, dubbed the Marina VP, a direct reference to Vanden Plas, played a leading role in the final design of the Morris Ital. Saloon and estate models were produced, and the new vehicles were launched in June 1980. There were no two-door (coupé) versions made.

Despite the external restyling, which resulted in a changed grille, headlamp indicator and front bumper arrangement, as well as revisions to the rear including the boot lid, which had a different profile as well as redesigned lighting and a larger black bumper, links to the Morris Marina parentage remained. L, HL and HLS saloon and estate models were available.

The new 1.3 A plus engine was used for the first time within British Leyland with the

Morris Ital 1.3 HL, with 1275 A plus 'A' series engine.

Ital. It later went on to be used in the Metro. The 1.7 engine used in the Mark III models continued in use with a four-speed gearbox as standard and an automatic three-speed Borg-Warner as an option. There were few changes to the other main mechanical components though the car was used as a test bed for new technology including flexible and solid printed circuit boards and improved manual gearboxes.

In October 1980 additional models were added to the range. 2.0-litre HLS saloon and estate versions became available with an automatic gearbox. These utilised the 2-litre version of the O Series engine. No manual gearbox models were available. Further

Morris Ital 1.3 HL instrument layout.

Morris Ital HLS instrument layout.

revisions occurred in November 1981. While L, HL and HLS models remained, changes occurred to the seating and trim materials, the standard equipment available and external chrome facings.

Major changes to the Ital models occurred in September 1982 when further mechanical and trim upgrades were introduced. At the same time production moved exclusively to Longbridge, thus ending the production of Morris cars at Cowley in Oxford. The model range was redesignated as follows: 1.3 SL, 1.3 SLX, 1.7 SL, 1.7 SLX saloons, 1.3 SL, 1.7 SL and 1.7 SLX estates. Entry level L models and the 2.0-litre cars had been discontinued in May 1982. The main changes to the vehicles centred on the introduction of telescopic front dampers, revisions to the rear springs, improved sound proofing, and altered levels of interior and exterior trim. With relatively few amendments the Morris Ital models remained in production until 1984. The last models to be produced were the estate models which remained in production until the arrival of the Austin Montego estate.

There was to be a last hurrah for the Ital in China. Within a year of the last Ital leaving the production line at Longbridge, the Ital presses and supporting plant for producing bodyshells was moved to China where it was modified to produce four variants of a vehicle which

Gearchange layout (all Itals).

Chinese Huandu CAC6430 based on the Morris Ital.

was initially designated as the Huandu model 9105. Essentially these were estate and van versions of the Ital powered by different engines and fitted with alternative suspension parts. In production they were classed as CAC 6430 models. Production in China continued until 1999.

Standard equipment on introduction included an alternator, water temperature gauge, trip mileage recorder, heater/demister with two-speed fan, face level ventilation, dipping rear view mirror, two-speed wipers, heated rear window, inertia reel seatbelts, hazard warning lights, reversing lights, rear fog lights, driver's door mirror, rear mud flaps, and, for the estate, a rear wiper/washer. HL had in addition a radio, a clock, cigarette lighter, glove box light, centre console, reclining front seats, passenger grab handles, boot light and body side moulding. HLS in addition to HL had a tachometer, intermittent windscreen wipe, front head rests, front door bins, rear seat centre armrest, passenger door mirror, tinted glass and a vinyl roof (saloon).

PRODUCTION NUMBERS: 1980, 51,274, 1981, 54,910, 1982, 33,572, 1983, 26,753, 1984, 8,707. Total 175,216.

PRICES ON INTRODUCTION: July 1980 four-door saloons 1.3L £3736, 1.3 HL £3980, 1.3 HLS £4396, 1.7 L £3961, HL £4205, HLS £4642. Estates 1.3L £4200, 1.7L £4427, 1.7HL £4671, 1.7HLS £5048.

PRICES OCTOBER 1982: four-door saloons. 1.3 SL £3998, 1.3 SLX £4498 1.7 SLX £4698 Estates. 1.3 SL £4747, 1.7 SL £4948, 1.7 SLX £5198.

COLOURS (1980): Ermine White, Vermilion Red, Pageant Blue, Applejack, Russet Brown, Champagne, Sand Glow, Snapdragon and the following metallics, Silver, Oyster, Denim Blue.

COLOURS (1983): Arum White, Champagne Beige, Cinnabar Red, Monza Red, Emberglow Red, Primula Yellow, Clove Brown, Eclipse Blue, Black and the following metallics, Silver Leaf, Cashmere Gold, Oporto Red, Opaline Green, Zircon Blue, Moonraker Blue.

ENGINE: All four-cylinder, 1.3 OHV, bore 70.61mm, stroke 81.28mm, 1275cc (77.8in3). Maximum bhp 60.8 at 5400rpm. SU HIF44 carburettor. 1.7 OHC, bore 84.5mm, stroke 75.87mm, 1700cc (103.7in[3]). Maximum bhp 77 at 5180rpm. SU HIF6 carburettor. 2.0 OHC, bore 84.5mm, stroke 89mm, 1994cc (121.7in[3]), maximum bhp 90 at 3250rpm. SU HIF6 carburettor.

GEARBOX: Four-speed all synchromesh, floor-mounted gearchange. Ratios: 1.3, top 3.89, third 5.56, second 8.208, first 13.265, reverse 14.589, 1.7, top 3.64, third 4.768, second 7.025, first 11.32, reverse 12.45, 2.0 top 3.27, second 4.74, first 7.825, reverse 6.847.

REAR AXLE: Hypoid bevel, ratio 1.3 3.89:1, 1.7 3.64:1, 2.0 3.270:1.

BRAKES: All models, dual line, power assisted, 9.79in front discs, rear 8in drums.

STEERING: Rack and pinion.

TYRES: 155 x 13.

SUSPENSION: Front: Independent, torsion bar, hydraulic arm shock absorbers. Rear: Semi-elliptic leaf springs, telescopic shock absorbers, front and rear anti-roll bars on saloons.

DIMENSIONS/WEIGHT: Saloon: **length**: 14ft 2.98in (4.34m); **width**: 5ft 4.41in (1.64m); **height**: 4ft 7.83in (1.42m); **wheelbase**: 8ft (2.438m); **track**: front and rear 4ft 4in (1.321m); **ground clearance**: 6.2in (15.75cm); **turning circle**: 31ft (9.45m); estate: as saloon except **length**: 14ft 4.36in (4.38m). Saloon: **weight**: 18cwt 1qtr 26lb (939kg); estate: 19cwt 1qtr 25lb (989kg).

CAPACITIES: Fuel: 11.5 gallons (52.3 litres). Boot: saloon 12.9ft[3], estate 31.4ft[3] or 58.4ft[3] with rear seat folded down.

Morris car-derived commercial vehicles

Morris commercial vehicles represented a sizeable proportion of the total number of Morris vehicles produced. Car-derived light commercial vehicles proved popular, and were produced in sizeable numbers. Sales of Morris light commercial vehicles were dominated in the late 1920s and throughout the 1930s by 5cwt van models based on the Morris Minor and the Morris

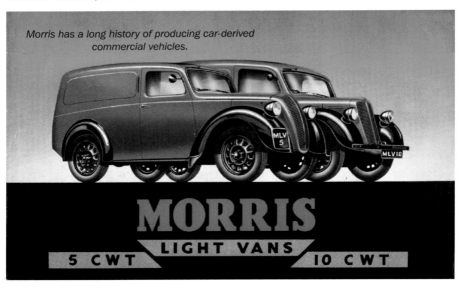

Morris has a long history of producing car-derived commercial vehicles.

PUBLICATION No. NEL.149

Eight. These proved popular with proprietors of small businesses as well as newly emerging fleet users. Morris vehicles proved popular with the General Post Office which ordered thousands of vans for its Telephone Engineer and Royal Mail fleets. Other Morris models of this era included slightly larger 8cwt and 10cwt Morris vans, and the Morris Series II 10cwt model introduced in 1935, which was also available as a truck with detachable wooden sides.

In the immediate postwar years the Morris Y-type van, first introduced in 1940, met the needs of those requiring a 10cwt light van, while the Morris Z-type, 5cwt model based on the Morris Eight fulfilled the needs of those requiring a smaller, more economical vehicle for business use. Following the first postwar Motor Show held in London in 1948, when the new Morris Oxford MO and Morris Minor Series MM models were showcased, light commercials in the guise of the 10cwt Morris Cowley and the 5cwt Morris Minor heralded a new era and large-scale production of car-derived commercials. Throughout the 1950s, aided by a growing reputation for reliability and economical motoring, Morris vehicles such as Morris Minor vans became established as fleet vehicles with prestigious organisations, including the General Post Office. 1960 saw

the first of the Alec Issigonis-designed Mini car-derived variants, with 5cwt Austin and Morris vans and pick-ups joining the range. Half-ton Austin and Morris vans based on the Austin A55 were produced from 1962, and there were even Austin-badged Morris Minor vans and pick-ups from 1968. When the Morris Minor was phased out in 1971 it was replaced by the Morris Marina. 7cwt and 10cwt van and pick-up models were added to the range in 1972. These commercial variants were later designated as Morris 440 and 575 vans and pick-ups. In 1982 the Ital took on the mantle, and, in the same year, Morris-badged Metro vans were added to the range. However, production of the Morris Metro vans was shortlived. When production of the Ital commercials ended in 1984 it signalled the end of the Morris marque. Optimists who lived in hope that at some point the Morris name would once again grace a new model were given fresh hope in 2019, when plans were revealed promising a new electric Morris JE-Type vehicle based on the original J-Type van by 2021.

Morris MCV half-ton van and pick-up

The Morris (MCV) half-ton (10cwt) van and pick-up models were introduced in March

Morris MCV half-ton pick-up (left) alongside a Morris Series III half-ton pick-up.

667 XUL

The series of commercial vehicles based on the Morris Oxford series MO were generally referred to as the Cowley van and pick-up.

1950. These were the first new postwar Morris light commercial vehicles to be announced, and, in keeping with previous light commercials, like the Z-type, they carried on the prewar tradition of car-based commercial vehicles. They were based on the Morris Oxford Series MO saloon that was announced in 1948 and marketed as the Cowley van and pick-up. They retained Morris badging on the bonnet.

The cab used the forward half of the Oxford MO body, but, by cutting it behind the B pillars, the strength of the monocoque body was lost. Therefore, the commercials reverted to a chassis layout using a mild steel frame with box sections that extended from the engine bay to the rear of the vehicle. The outriggers curved outwards and upwards to accept the rear spring shackles and clear the rear axle. Rigidity was provided by a transverse beam through which the propshaft was aligned. The chassis was manufactured in Coventry while the body panels were made by Nuffield Metal Products.

The rear panels, for both the van and pick-up, were bolted to the chassis and the cab, and were detachable. The front half was virtually identical to the Morris Oxford Series MO saloon apart from the front grille, which, on the commercial vehicles was always a painted version of the original Mazak grille used when the Morris Oxford Series MO saloon was introduced. The commercials also utilised the 1476cc side-valve engine and gearbox used in the Series MO saloon. Internally the dashboard was like that used in the saloon. The bench seat used in the saloon was available on export models as standard. Home market van models were supplied with a single driver's seat as standard, but a passenger

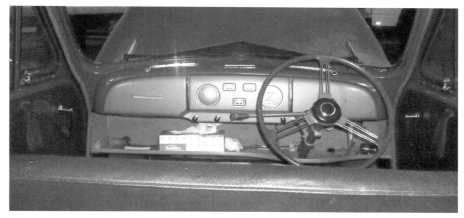

25 JMT is a time warp garage find which has been sympathetically recommissioned to its current excellent condition.

seat or a bench seat could be specified as an optional extra. The cab had rubber floor covering appropriate to the utilitarian use of these vehicles. The interior trimming was only available in brown Vynide, a feature set to be replicated in other Morris light commercials for many years. Early models had black wheels and hub caps, black bumpers, and a single black external mirror for the driver mounted on the windscreen pillar. Later models had plain chrome hubcaps, without an 'M' motif, and chrome bumpers. Both van and pick-up models were supplied with a basic tool kit which included a jack. Any mechanical improvements made to the Series MO saloons while they were in production were usually replicated on the light commercial vehicles. The MCV half-ton (10cwt) range remained in production until September 1956 when they were replaced by the Series III half-ton (10cwt) van and pick-ups based on the Cowley 1500/ Morris Oxford Series III range.

PRODUCTION NUMBERS: Vans 30,100. Pick-ups 10,600.
COSTS: 1950 van (painted) £492. Pick-up (painted) £486. Cost to paint in one of four standard colours £6. Extra passenger seat £4 15s. Note. A basic chassis cab was available with or without a cab back. This was supplied in primer.
COLOURS: 1950 Platinum Grey, Beige, Railly Blue, Dark Green. 1956 Clarendon Grey, Empire Green, Sandy Beige.

117

OPTIONAL EXTRAS: Heater, passenger seat or bench seat, canvas tilt and hoops (pick-up).
ENGINE: Four-cylinder side-valve. Bore 73.5mm stroke 87mm capacity 1476.53cc. Maximum bhp 40.5. SU-H2 (1¼in) carburettor.
GEARBOX: Four-speed with synchromesh on all gears except first. Steering column change. Ratios: fourth 5.620, third 8.470, second 12.670, first 21.410.
REAR AXLE: Hypoid three-quarter floating. Ratio: 5.625: 1 (8/45).
BRAKES: Lockheed hydraulic front and rear 9in diameter drums. Handbrake located under dash.
STEERING: Rack and pinion. 3 turns lock-to-lock.
TYRES: 6.00-15.
SUSPENSION: Front: Independent with torsions bars and links. Rear: Semi-elliptic leaf springs. Hydraulic shock absorbers front and rear.
DIMENSIONS: Van: **length**: 14ft (4.63m); **height**: 6ft 2in (1.800m); **width**: 5ft 9in (1.752m). Pick-up: **length**: 14ft (4.63m); **height**: (cab roof) 5ft 8in (1.72m); **width**: 5ft 9in (1.752).
CAPACITIES: Fuel: 12 gallons (54.5 litres). Loading capacity: Van 120ft³ (3.4m³); pick-up 135ft³ (3.8m³) with the passenger seat removed.

1954 van originally exported to New Zealand; now back in the UK.

Morris Minor O-type quarter-ton van and pick-up
(More commonly referred to as Series II commercials)

The first Morris Minor car-derived commercials did not appear until May 1953 when the 'O' Type quarter-ton vans and pick-up models were announced. While instantly recognisable as Morris Minors, their specification differed in many respects from the saloon and convertible models in the range. The principal difference was the fact that the van and pick-up bodies were mounted on an all-steel separate chassis. Other external difference included a bonnet devoid of side body mouldings, a shorter painted front bumper, painted window frames with fixed quarter lights initially, the absence of chrome inserts in the windscreen rubber, a painted centre windscreen pillar, and black-painted windscreen wiper arms. A black, externally fitted mirror was fixed to the driver's side windscreen pillar as standard, and a specially adapted external Lucas trafficator box could be fitted to ensure the trafficators were visible past the extended width of the van body. Internally the trim specification featured a rubber floor covering, brown seats, plain brown door cards, and a

Early (top) and late fascia arrangements for O-type Morris Minor commercials.

three-piece Rexine-covered headlining. On delivery only a driver's seat was supplied as standard, with the passenger seat having to specified as an optional extra. Mechanically the commercials used the same A series 803cc engine and corresponding gearbox as used in the rest of the range. In addition, a low-compression engine was offered.

Yes, those are rubber wings on the Post Office engineer's van.

The Post Office, keen to use the new vehicles, placed a large order, and, in an effort to reduce costs, insisted on changed specifications from standard production vehicles. Most notable on the early Post Office engineers' vans and some mail vans was the use of rubber wings with externally fitted headlamps on the top, an opening front windscreen arrangement, and roof-mounted windscreen wipers. Many other detailed changes were specified for these and subsequent GPO vehicles.

Standard production vans and pick-up models followed the changes which occurred

in the rest of the Series II range, and, in 1954, the front grille arrangement along with the revised fascia was introduced. The Series II models remained in production until 1956 when the Morris Minor 1000 models were introduced. The commercial variants, though, were designated as Series III models.

PRODUCTION NUMBERS: Series II vans and pick-up 1953-1956: approximately 49,226.
COST: 1955 van £392 (painted) £387 (unpainted) pick-up £386 (painted) £381 unpainted. Options included a cab with or without a cab back painted or unpainted. Extras: Bucket seat £7. Pick-up tilt £14.
COLOURS:1953-55 Platinum Grey, Dark Green, Azure Blue, Beige. 1955-56 Sandy Beige Clarendon Grey, Empire Green, Azure Blue. Vehicles could be supplied in primer for customers to provide their own colour scheme or livery.
Specifications where different from other Morris Minor Series II models.
SUSPENSION: Rear suspension semi-elliptic rear springs with rubber mounting controlled by telescopic hydraulic shock absorbers with anti-sway mountings.
OPTIONAL EXTRAS: Heater, passenger seat

(home market), canvas tilt with hoops (pick-up).
DIMENSIONS: Van: **length**: 11ft 10⅜in (3.62m); **width**: 5ft ½in (1.54m); **height**: 5ft 5⅞in (1.67m). Pick-up: **length**: 11ft 10⅜in (3.62m); **width**: 5ft ½in (1.54m); **height**: 5ft ½in (1.54m); **height to top of tailgate**: 3ft 6in (1.07m); **overall height with tilt erected**: 5ft 3½in (1.61m).
CAPACITIES: Van load space 78ft³ (2.2m³).

Morris Minor Series III quarter-ton van and pick-up
When the new Morris 1000 (948cc) models were announced in 1956 the commercial variants were designated Series III. They acquired the same mechanical upgrades as the rest of the range, and most of the changes made to the frontal area of the cars including the full-width single-piece windscreen, narrower windscreen pillars and the changed roof pressing. Exceptions were the bonnet, badging, and the front bumper arrangement. The van and pick-up bonnet did not have the side mouldings used on the rest of the range, and the badging consisted of the bonnet flash and winged badge first used on the Series MM cars

Morris van and pick-up (right). Small rear windows were a feature of Series III vans.

in 1948. A further distinguishing feature was the shorter bumper blade which did not extend to the full width of the bumper valance. The van back and pick-up bed remained unchanged from the earlier Series II models. Internal trim differed from the cars in that only plain brown door cards, brown upholstery, and a black rubber floor covering were available. In keeping with most commercial vehicles, the passenger

seat was an optional extra. A spare wheel was supplied. In the van it was stowed on the passenger side of the rear compartment behind where the passenger seat was fitted. On the pick-up it could either be stowed inside the cab on the passenger side if a seat was not fitted or externally on the cab back.

Morris Minor Series V 6cwt van and pick-up
Austin Series C van and pick-up
When the 1098cc engine was introduced to the Morris Minor range in September 1962, the Series III designation for commercial vehicles remained unchanged

Badge engineering. Austin bonnet badge and marque-defining crinkle grille identify this as an Austin Morris Minor!

in contemporary sales brochures. However, other factory publications denote the 6cwt vans and pick-ups as Series V. Accompanying the larger engine were a larger 7¼in clutch and revised front brakes, which now featured 8in front drums. Other changes included a new two-spoke steering wheel and improved visibility courtesy of larger rear windows in the van doors. 1964 brought further changes across the model range, and, in January 1965, the light commercials acquired a new-style fascia complete with an anodised backing panel, new speedometer,

and revised toggle switches. A major development occurred in 1968 when Series C Austin-badged 6cwt versions of the Morris Minor van and pick-up were announced. Differences were limited to Austin badging on the bonnet and the steering wheel, the fitting of a traditional Austin crinkle-type grille panel, and the introduction of an eight-leaf spring arrangement on all vans and pick-ups. In April 1968 an 8cwt payload option was added to both the Morris and Austin. This was accompanied by changes to the suspension, with stronger seven-leaf

Last post. One of the last Morris Minor Royal Mail vans, pictured in appropriate surroundings.

springs being introduced along with wider 4½ J wheels, stronger front suspension uprights and steering levers. Production switched to Adderley Park, Birmingham, and it was here that the last Morris Minor- and Austin-badged vans and pick-ups were built in 1971.

PRODUCTION NUMBERS: Total production Series II, Series III, Series V, Austin Series C 326,627.
COSTS: 1960 Series III quarter-ton van (painted in factory colour) £385. Pick-up £378. 1970 Series V 6cwt van (painted in factory colour) £438. 8cwt van £464. Series V 6cwt pick-up (painted in factory colour) £471. 8 cwt pick-up £497.
COLOURS: Series III 1956-1962: Sandy Beige, Empire Green, Blue, Clarendon Grey, Dark Green, Connaught Green, Frilford Grey, Birch Grey, Yukon Grey, Pearl Grey, Rose Taupe, Almond Green, Dove Grey, Old English White.

Morris Series III half-ton (10cwt) commercials

The Series III half-ton (10cwt) van and pick-up models were introduced in late October 1956, and became available at dealerships from November 1956. They replaced the previous Morris Commercial Vehicles (MCV) half-ton vans and pick-ups based on the Oxford Series MO produced between 1952 and 1956.

The specification of the MCV Series III vans and pick-ups incorporated features from the Cowley 1200 introduced in July 1954 and the restyled Cowley 1500 introduced in October 1956. Although never officially named as such, they were unofficially identified by the public as Cowley vans and pick-ups. Like the Cowley 1200, both models had a rounded bonnet, however, the bonnet was unique in that it did not have an air-vent, nor did it use the restyled fluted bonnet badge of the Cowley 1500 and Oxford Series III. The Morris badge on the front of the bonnet was retained, but there was no 'Cowley' designation on the front wings, bonnet, or anywhere else.

The commercial models shared many mechanical features with the Cowley 1500 including the 1489cc OHV engine, albeit with variations to gearbox and axle ratios. Other shared features included the dashboard, steering wheel, plain headlamp rims, painted

Morris Series III half-ton van and pick-up models remained in production from 1956 to 1960.

door window surrounds, opening quarter light windows and indicators. Items typical of lower specification commercial vehicles included a single option of brown Vynide interior trim, a single driver's seat as standard on home market van models, with the option of an additional passenger seat or a bench-type front seat, and more practical rubber floor

coverings. A bench seat was standard on export models. Distinctive external features included black-painted wing mirrors mounted close to the windscreen, a plain windscreen rubber devoid of embellishment, a nearside fuel filler and an exhaust system which discharged from the side.

The option of a chassis cab was retained. Vehicles could be supplied in primer for individual or fleet buyers to add their own livery.

Production continued until October 1960.

Left-hand drive interior.

Instrument layout. The clock and heater controls were blanked off on commercial models.

Gearchange layout on introduction.

PRODUCTION NUMBERS: Vans, pick-ups and chassis cabs 16,177.

COST 1956: Van £610, pick-up £599, additional passenger seat £8, bench seat (van) £10, canvas tilt (pick-up) £20.

COLOURS 1956-1960: Clarendon Grey, Birch Grey, Empire Green, Dark Green, Sandy Beige. (In 1957 painting in the factory colours available for that year was £5 10s).

OPTIONAL EXTRAS: Heater, windscreen washers, passenger seat or bench seat (van) and canvas tilt (pick-up).

ENGINE: Four-cylinder OHV, bore 73.025mm, stroke 88.9mm 1489cc (90.88in³). Maximum bhp 50. SU H2 (1¼in) carburettor.

GEARBOX: Four-speed with synchromesh on all gears except first. Column then floor change. Ratios top 5.125, third 7.640, second 12.320, first 20.220, reverse 26.440.

REAR AXLE: Hypoid bevel, three-quarter floating, ratio 5.125:1 (8/41).

BRAKES: Lockheed hydraulic drum 10in. Handbrake to rear brakes located between seat edge and door.

TYRES: 6.00 x 15.

SUSPENSION: Front independent torsion bar with hydraulic shock absorbers. Rear half-elliptic springs with hydraulic shock absorbers.

STEERING: Rack and pinion 3.125 turns lock-to-lock. Turning circle 10.74-10.82m.

DIMENSIONS: Van: **length**: 14ft ⅜in (4.270m); **height**: 6ft 1½in (1.870m); **width**: 5ft 8in (1.778m); **weight**: 23.15cwt (1175kg). Pick-up: **length**: 14ft ⅜in (4.270m); **height**: 5ft 3¼in (1.600m); **width**: 5ft 8in (1.778m); **weight**: 23cwt (1181kg).

CAPACITIES: Loading area, van 120-138ft³, pick-up 50-120ft³. Fuel 9.88 gallons (45 litres).

Morris Mini van and pick-up

Commercial variants of the Austin and Morris Mini did not appear until a year after the Austin Se7en and Morris Mini Minor saloons were launched. Quarter-ton Morris Mini van models were introduced in June 1960, with pick-up versions first appearing in March 1961. Mechanical specifications mirrored those of their saloon counterparts, though the 5cwt commercials had a 4in longer wheelbase and a longer body than the saloons. The battery positioning was different, being behind the driver's seat as opposed to being in the boot on the saloon, and the spare wheel was stowed beneath the payload floor behind the passenger seat (when fitted). Maximum storage capacity was a useful 58ft³ in the van and the pick-up bed could be extended to 6ft when the tail gate, which had a hinged number plate, was in the down position. Competitively priced at launch, the vans in particular sold well. Cost saving features included a one-piece painted grille panel, single choice upholstery colour and light grey rubber floor coverings. An interesting difference was the fact that vans had split rear quarter bumpers while the pick-up had a single-piece rear bumper fitted until 1969. The 848cc was standard on all models, though in 1967 at the time when Mk II models were introduced, a 998cc engine was made available as an option on the commercial vehicles. After 1969, in tandem with the rest of the range, the van

A one-piece painted grille was a distinctive feature of commercial variants of the Mini.

and pick-up ceased to be badged as Austin or Morris, though they continued to be listed in Morris sales brochures and price listings right up to their eventual demise in 1983. From 1978 they became known as Mini 95 models, the '95' designation relating to the gross weight of 0.95 tons. By this time, although the rear light arrangement was altered, neither the van nor the pick-up models had changed much in terms of their basic design since their inception.

PRODUCTION NUMBERS: Pick-ups 1961-1983 (Austin, Morris and Mini 95) 58,179. Morris-badged pick-ups 12,577. Vans 1960-1983 (Austin, Morris and Mini 95). Total production 521,494.

This 1960 van finished in Whitehall Beige was the eighth off the production line. Instrumentation was the same as the basic Mk I Morris Mini Minor.

COST ON INTRODUCTION: 1960 Morris quarter-ton Mini van £360. Morris Mini quarter-ton pick-up 1961 £360. Cost in 1969 (last year badged as a Morris) Mini quarter-ton delivery van including windscreen washer and interior light in primer £435. In standard colour £445. Pick-up in primer £435. In standard colour £443. Optional extra available van and pick-up: Passenger seat, recirculatory heater, front over-riders, pick-up tilt. A 998cc engine was available at extra cost of £20 for both models.

COLOURS 1961: Whitehall Beige, Tweed Grey, Willow Green all with tan seats.

OPTIONAL EXTRAS 1962: Van passenger seat £6. Pick-up tilt (supplied but not fitted) £10. Both models heater, front over-riders, windscreen washer.

Mechanical specifications were as for 848cc Mini saloons with the following exceptions.

DIMENSIONS: Van: **length**: 10ft 9⅞in (3.30m); **width**: 4ft 7½in (1.41m); **height**: 4ft 6½in (1.38m). Pick-up: **length**: 10ft 10½in (3.32m); **width**: 4ft 7½in; **height**: 4ft 5½in (1.36m).

CAPACITIES: Van payload capacity: 46ft^3 (1.3m^3) with an additional 12ft^3 (0.34m^3) with passenger seat removed. Pick-up: 30ft^3 (0.85m^3) up to the waistline. Fuel: 6 gallons (27 litres).

Morris half-ton van and pick-up 1962-1971

The Morris half-ton van and pick-up models introduced in 1962 were essentially badge-engineered Austin models. The Austin A50 Cambridge saloon introduced in 1954 provided the basis for an Austin half-ton van based on the upgraded A55 of 1957. Van versions introduced in February 1957 were followed by a pick-up in May 1957. When face-lifted models appeared in 1962, they were joined by 'new' Morris equivalent models. In terms of body styling and mechanical components they were identical apart from the traditional marque front grilles and the badging on the bonnet and on the steering wheel.

Early Morris models were powered by

Morris half-ton van. Dating from 1972 this is one of the last to be produced.

the 1489cc OHV B series engine. A higher compression version could be specified. The van was a spacious vehicle of all-steel construction incorporating a one-piece steel roof and body sides, while the pick-up had all-steel ribbed inner panels for extra strength and a tailgate constructed of double steel panels held horizontally by anchor chains. Van capacity provided 110ft^3 (3.12m^3) of load space, and the rear compartment was easily accessed by large rear doors with spring loaded checks built into concealed hinges to secure them in the open position. The higher roof line, lower loading height and flat-topped wheelarches combined to provide an readily accessible and useable loading area. Instrumentation and interior fitments mirrored those of the saloon models except for the seating. In vans a driver's seat was supplied as standard with the passenger seat available as

Proven and reliable workhorses!

an optional extra, while on the pick-up a bench seat was supplied as standard. Upholstery was supplied in black with Dove Grey piping. Durable floor covering in the form of a rubber mat was fitted in the cab.

In 1963 both models were upgraded when the engine size was increased. A 1622cc OHV engine was fitted, and several other mechanical upgrades were introduced including changes to the wheel and tyre sizes. The models continued in production until 1972 when they were phased out following the introduction of the Morris Marina commercials.

Sun Tor conversion
on Morris half-ton van
with duo-tone paint
finish and owner-added
exterior sun visor.

COST 1971: Delivery van £690 (in red primer), £702 (in standard colour). Chassis/scuttle £604 (less doors), £634 (with doors). Pick-up £695 (in red primer), £707 (in standard colour). Chassis/cab (with bench seat and back panel) £695 (in red primer), £669 in standard colour.

COLOURS 1962: Horizon Blue, Tweed Grey, Farina Grey, Willow Green.

OPTIONAL EXTRAS 1962: Passenger seat on van, heater and demister, over-riders.

ENGINE: Four-cylinder in line OHV, bore 2.875in (73.025mm) stroke 3.5in (89.0mm). Cubic capacity 1489cc (90.88in^3). Maximum bhp 47 @4100rpm. Compression ratio 7.2: 1 (8.3:1 available). Zenith downdraught carburettor.

GEARBOX: Four-speed column gearchange. Ratios: fourth 1.000, third 1.490, second 2.402, first 3.945, reverse 5.159.

REAR AXLE: Ratio 4.875:1 (8/39).

STEERING: Cam and peg.

SUSPENSION: Front independent with wishbones, coil springs and shock absorbers; rear semi-elliptic leaf springs with shock absorbers and stabilizing bar, lever-type shock absorbers.

BRAKES: Girling hydraulic, two leading shoes at front, 9in (0.23m) diameter x 1½in (0.044m) wide.

TYRES: 6.00-15 tubeless tyres.

DIMENSIONS: Van: **length**: 14ft ¾in (4.29m); **width**: 5ft 2½in (1.59m); **height**: 5ft 8¾in (1.75m). Pick-up: **length**: 14ft ¾in (4.29m);

width: 5ft 2½in (1.59m); **height**: 5ft 3¼in (1.61m).
CAPACITIES: Fuel: 8¼ gallons (37.5 litres). Load capacity van 110ft³ (3.12m³). Specification changes 1962.
ENGINE: Four-cylinder OHV, bore 3.00in (76.20mm), stroke 3.5 in (89.0mm) cubic capacity 1622cc (98.98in³). Maximum bhp 56 @4500rpm. Compression ratio 7.2: 1. SU HS2 carburettor.
GEARBOX: Four-speed column gearchange. Ratios: fourth 1.000, third 1.490, second 2.402, first 3.945, reverse 5.159.
REAR AXLE: Three-quarter floating rear axle. Ratio 4.55 :1 (9/41).

Morris Marina 7cwt and 10cwt van and 10cwt pick-up

The first commercial variants based on the Morris Marina were announced on the 1st August 1972, and displayed at the Earls Court Motor in October 1972. 7cwt and 10cwt vans were on show, but it was not until 1973 that the 10cwt pick-up model

made an appearance. The Marina vans were replacements for the Morris Minor 6cwt and 8cwt models and the Austin and Morris car-derived half-ton vans and pick-ups originally based on the Austin A55 models. At launch three variants of the 7cwt van were available: standard van with a choice of 1098cc or 1275cc A series engine, and a deluxe model fitted with the 1275cc engine and marketed as a 1300 model. When launched the pick-up was offered as a 1300 deluxe model only. The commercials shared much of the front end styling, pressed steel panels and many of the mechanical components of the Morris Marina saloons. The load-space floor on the vans was swaged and incorporated a lip at its front end to prevent the load sliding forward. The front section of the load space passed over the driving compartment floor wells thus creating a useful storage space on the nearside for the spare wheel, and on the offside for the tool-kit and spare wheel changing equipment. Mechanical differences included the rear suspension

Early promotional brochure.

Single binnacle instrument layout was a feature in early models.

and changed axle ratios. An uprated suspension system, which included four-leaf semi-elliptic springs, rubber pads to dampen road noise, and rear telescopic shock absorbers, was adopted to cope with the additional loading capacity. Axle ratios differed between the 7cwt and 10cwt vans (7cwt 4.111:1, 10cwt 4.556:1). To the

Marina-based Sun Tor conversion.

Morris Marina 575 pick-up.

Morris Marina 440 instrument layout and interior.

rear of the vehicle the light clusters were recessed into the bodywork and the number plate lamps were located beneath the rear floor sill to reduce the risk of damage. The Marina vans were regarded as large by UK car-derived commercial standards, with 88ft^3 available to the rear and 104ft^3 possible with the passenger seat removed.

PRODUCTION NUMBERS 1972-1980: Approximately 150,000.

PRICE ON INTRODUCTION: 7cwt vans, standard trim, 1098cc £665, 1275cc £695. Deluxe trim 1275cc £735. 10cwt van 1275cc £775.

COLOURS: 1975. Tahiti Blue, Glacier White, Cumulus Grey, primer.

ENGINE: Four-cylinder OHV, bore 2543in (64.58mm) stroke 3.296 in (83.72) capacity 1098cc (67in^3). Maximum bhp 46.5

@5150rpm. Single SU H4 carburettor. Four-cylinder OHV, bore 2.78in (70.61), stroke 3.20in (81.28mm), capacity 1275cc (77.8in^3). Maximum bhp 57 @5500rpm. Single SU HS4 carburettor.

GEARBOX: Four-speed, all synchromesh. Ratios: fourth 1.000, third 1.433, second 2.112, first 3.142, reverse 3.753:1.

REAR AXLE: Semi-floating hypoid gear drive. Ratios with 1098cc engine 4.55: 1, with 1275cc engine 4.111:1.

STEERING: Rack and pinion.

SUSPENSION: Front: Independent, torsion bars and lever arm hydraulic dampers. Rear: Semi-elliptic leaf springs and telescopic hydraulic dampers.

BRAKES: 7cwt van: Hydraulic with 8in (0.20m) diameter drums all round. Two leading shoes at front, leading and trailing at rear. 10cwt van and pick-up: Hydraulic 9in (0.23m) diameter drums all round. Two leading shoes at front, leading and trailing at rear. Brake servo.

TYRES: 7cwt van: 155SR-13 radial ply tyres. 10cwt van and pick-up: 155SR-13 reinforced radial tyres.

DIMENSIONS: Van: **length**: 13ft 9.5in

(4.21m); **width**: 5ft 4.4in (1.64m); **height**: 7cwt 5ft 2.4in (1.58m), 10cwt 5ft 2.6in (1.59m). 10cwt pick-up: **length**: 13ft 9in (4.19m); **width**: 5ft 4.4in (1.64m); **height**: 4ft 9in (1.45m).
CAPACITIES: Fuel: 11½ gallons (52 litres). Load space: van 88ft³ (2.49m³), with passenger seat removed 104ft³ (2.94m³), pick-up 36ft³ (1.02m³).

Morris Marina 440 van and 575 van and pick-up

The Morris Marina commercial vehicle range was renamed following the introduction of the Marina Mk III in 1978. The 7cwt van was redesignated as the Morris 440 van, and the 10cwt van and pick-up models were identified as the Morris 575 van and pick-up. All models were fitted with the 1275cc A series engine, and other mechanical changes were introduced, including improved braking, revised carburation, and better engine cooling. The revised dashboard adopted in the Marina Mk III was fitted. Trim levels were altered with L level trim replacing the previous deluxe specification. However, in the case of the pick-up, the L level of trim was not available. Standard specification included, twin black door mirrors, one-piece front door glass, trimmed door panels, Zebra toughened windscreen and safety glass windows, driver and passenger seats, static seatbelts, full width floor mat, twin sun visors with docket pockets, two-speed electric fan heater and face level ventilation, interior mirror, hard rimmed steering wheel, and a PVC headlining. External features included a rolled section black front bumper and rear quarter bumpers as well as black plastic wheel nut covers and wheel trim centre caps. L specification added padded vinyl three-quarter door trim, door arm rests and trim door bins, inertia reel seatbelts, dipping rear view mirror, soft finish fascia crash roll, bright tape inserts in the bumpers, bright sill tread strips, and a cigar lighter.

Morris 440 van and Morris 575 van and pick-up main mechanical specification changes.
ENGINE: 1275cc engine with SU HF1

carburettor and viscous coupled cooling fan (440 and 575).
BRAKES: 440 model: Dual line hydraulically operated with servo assistance, 9.79in (248mm) discs at front with 8in (203mm) drum brakes at rear. 575 models: Dual line hydraulically operated with servo assistance, 9.7in (248mm) discs at front with 9in (248mm) drum brakes at rear.

Morris Ital 440 van and 575 van and pick-up

The transition from Morris Marina to Morris Ital commercial vehicles mirrored that of the saloon and estate models which had been launched in 1980. The difference was that the Morris Ital 440 and 575 van and pick-up models did not appear until October 1982. The main equipment and styling changes which occurred included revised front end styling with halogen headlamps and moulded wrap around bumpers, a saloon style fascia which included twin dial instrumentation, night-time illumination for heater controls and switches, improved acoustic insulation, and the addition of glove box lids and a passenger parcel shelf. Mechanically there were few changes, but the use of the A plus 1275cc engine introduced in 1980 continued. Standard and L trim specifications were carried forward with the L level of trim being applied to the 440 and 575 van models only. L levels of trim offered a four-spoke steering wheel (standard models had a two-spoke steering wheel), full width fabric seat facings, reclining front seats with a tip-forward

The Ital 440 and 575 were the last Morris models.

passenger seat, carpeting in the cab, courtesy light switches and a locking fuel cap. Established L trim items such as soft trimmed front door panels with armrests and door bins, inertia seatbelts and a cigarette lighter were all retained.

Following the end of saloon and estate car production of the Morris Ital in April 1984 production of the Morris Ital 440 and 575 vans and pick-ups continued for a time thus making them the last vehicles to carry the Morris name. No vehicles, commercial or otherwise, carried the Morris name beyond 1985.

COST 1983: 440 van £4248, 440L van £4424, van 575 £4610 ,van 575L £ 4782, pick-up 575L £4681 (all with 1275cc engine). **COLOURS 1983**: Arum White, Champagne Beige, Cinnabar Red, Monza Red, Emberglow Red, Primula Yellow, Clove Brown, Eclipse Blue, Black.

Instrument layout Ital 575. Centre console is a post production addition.

Changes to specification from preceding model.
ENGINE: A plus 1275cc OHV engine with 9:4:1 compression ratio. Increased bhp to 60.8 @5400rpm. SU HIF 44 carburettor.

Morris Metro van

The Morris Ital range of vehicles were destined to be the last to bear the Morris name. However for a short time the Morris name was assigned to commercial versions of the Austin Metro. Morris 1.0, 1.0L, 1.3 and 1.3L Metro vans were introduced in 1982. They had the distinction of being the last new car-derived vehicles to be assigned the Morris badge.

The Metro, which was launched in 1980 following a £275 million development programme had many innovative features, many of which were retained on the commercials. Key features included the economical but powerful A Plus engine, 12,000-mile service intervals, fuel efficient aerodynamic styling, saloon levels of equipment, comfortable seating and 45.7ft3 of load space which could be increased by removing the front passenger seat. Access to the rear load area was enhanced by the use of a gas assisted tailgate and tilt and slide front seats.

Standard equipment included trip recorder, warning lights including brake circuit failure, brake pad wear and low fluid levels, two-speed windscreen wipers with flick wipe facility, thermostatically controlled electric radiator cooling fan, and a rear fog guard lamp. In addition, fitted carpets in the cab and a fresh air heater/demister with two-speed fan and face level vents were included. L specification models also had reversing lamps, an electrically heated rear window, warning lights to indicate that the heated rear window was on and that the choke was in use, passenger sun visor, a drivers door bin and hounds-tooth check fabric seat facings instead of the vinyl seat covering fitted to the standard model. Optional extras included heated rear window (standard on L models), low-compression

Metro economy.
Metro handling. Metro quality.
Metro roominess.
Metro reliability.

The Metro van is here, sharing many of the advantages of Britain's best selling small car. And benefitting from the same advanced technology.

It comes with a massive 45.7 cu.ft. of carrying capacity.

And like all Metros, it should also keep its value better than many competitors.

Metro van comes with a choice of 1 litre and 1.3 litre engines and in two specifications. See it for yourself. And discover how driving for business can be every bit as enjoyable as driving for pleasure.

Very few Morris-badged Metro vans remain.

Instrument panel showing gearchange pattern.

(8.3: 1) 1.0 or 1.3 engine, laminated windscreen, push button radio/stereo cassette, rear wash wipe.

In addition, an easy-load floor (Unipart Part number GAC319) which provided a flat, boot sill height loading surface that allowed for easy handling and loading of heavy goods could be specified. It had the advantage of having two split rear floor sections with storage space underneath.

After the Morris name had been deleted from the range a number of revisions were made and the vans were then badged as Austin Metro 310 models. Following the establishment of the Rover Group in 1989 all subsequent vans were registered as Rovers and simply known as Metro vans. Production continued until 1991.

COST 1983: Morris 1.0 £3210, 1.0L £3529, 1.3 £3386, 1.3L £3705. Note. Customers wishing to have the low-compression engines could do so at no extra cost to these prices.
COLOURS: Base models: Ermine White, Champagne Beige, Nautilus Blue; L models: Primula Yellow, Cinnabar Red.
ENGINE: Four-cylinder transverse OHV 1.0-litre, bore 2.54in (64.58mm), stroke 3.0in (76.2mm), capacity 998cc (60.96in^3).

Maximum bhp 45 @5000rpm. Single carburettor. 1.3-litre, bore 2.78in (70.64mm), stroke 3.20in (81.28mm), capacity 1275cc (77.8in^3). Maximum bhp 60 @5200rpm. Single carburettor.
GEARBOX: Four-speed, all synchromesh. Ratios first 3.647, second 1.84, third 1.425, fourth 1.000, reverse 3.666:1. Final drive front-wheel drive. Ratio. (1.0) 3.647:1; (1.3) 3.44:1.
BRAKES: Dual line hydraulically operated with servo assistance on 1.3 models. 8.38in (213mm) diameter discs at front, 7in drums at the rear.
STEERING: Rack and pinion. Two-spoke steering wheel.
TYRES: (1.0) 135x12 radial ply tyres, (1.3) 155/70x12 radial ply tyres.
SUSPENSION: Front: Independent Hydragas springs, telescopic dampers anti-roll bar. Rear: Independent trailing arms, Hydragas springs with internal damping plus coil pre-loaded springs.
DIMENSIONS: **Length**: 11ft 2in (3.404m), **height**: 4ft 5.5in (1.359m); **width**: 5ft 1in (1.554m).
CAPACITIES: Fuel: 6.5 gallons (29.5 litres). Load area 45.7ft^3 (1.29m^3).

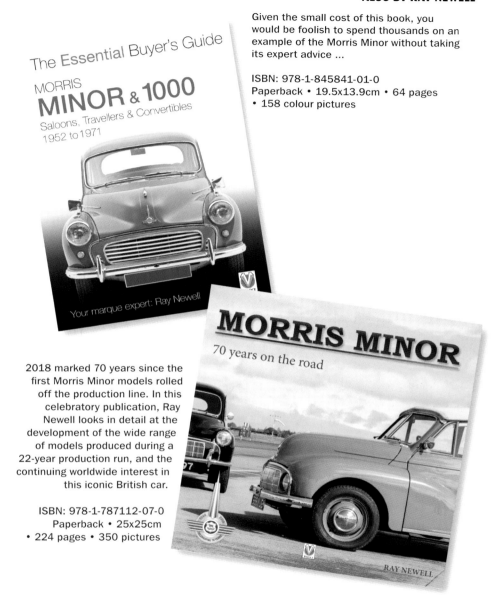

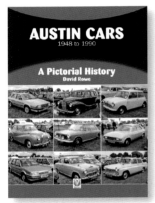

978-1-787112-19-3

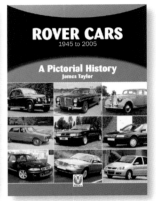

978-1-787116-09-2

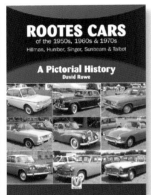

978-1-787114-43-2

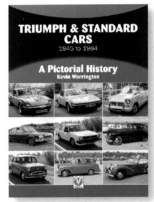

978-1-787110-77-9

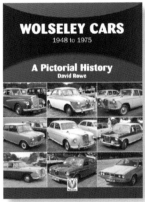

978-1-787110-78-6

For more information and price details, visit our website at www.veloce.co.uk
• email: info@veloce.co.uk • Tel: +44(0)1305 260068

Index

MORRIS CARS 1948 to 1984 – A Pictorial History